The
Bomb
Vessel

The bombardment of Bastia in Corsica, 6 November 1745, painting by Samuel Scott.

The bomb vessel, firing explosive shells or incendiary carcasses, was a powerful addition to the armoury of navies in what might be termed the coastal offence role. This bombardment was originally intended to support a local insurrection, and although the rebel forces did not coordinate their attack and the squadron withdrew, the town's defences were so damaged that it surrendered when the insurrectionists made a demonstration before the walls shortly afterwards. The bomb vessels are the typical ketch rigged craft of the period.

The Bomb Vessel

Shore Bombardment Ships
of the Age of Sail

Chris Ware

Illustrated with draughts from the collections
of the National Maritime Museum

Naval Institute Press

Annapolis, Maryland

© Chris Ware

First published in Great Britain in 1994 by
Conway Maritime Press,
an imprint of Brassey's (UK) Ltd,
33 John Street,
London WC1N 2AT

Published and distributed in the United States of America and Canada by
the Naval Institute Press,
118 Maryland Avenue, Annapolis, Maryland 21402-5035

Library of Congress Catalog Card No. 94-69302

ISBN 1-55750-071-1

All uncredited illustrations are from the collection of the National
Maritime Museum, Greenwich

Manufactured in Great Britain

Contents

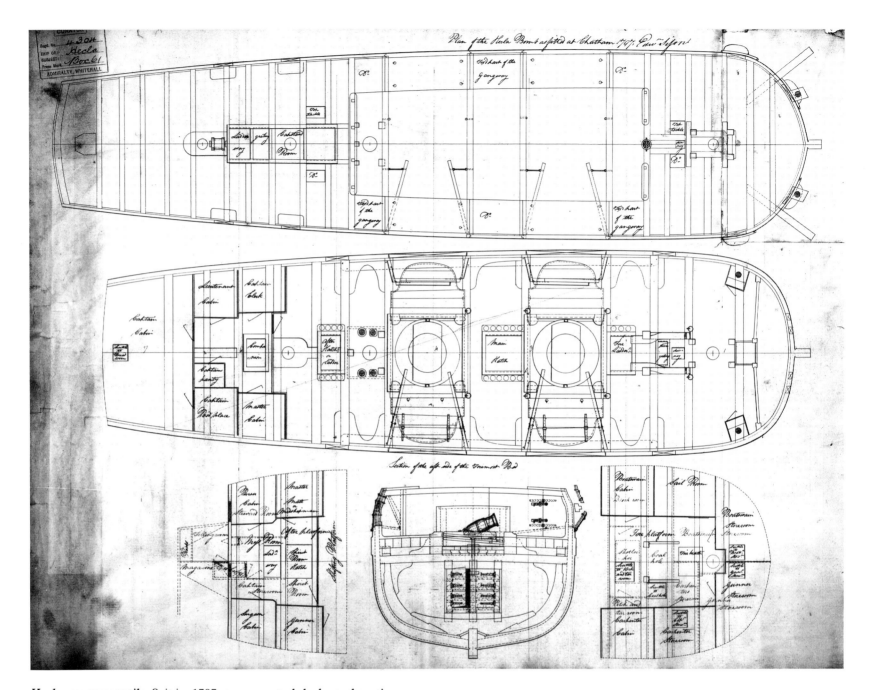

Hecla, ex mercantile *Scipio*, 1797, as converted decks and section

Bomb vessels were never built in large numbers, so 'standard' practice did not really exist as understood for larger warships. As a result, draughts tended to be more elaborate and more detailed, this plan being a prime example. The ship was one of seven merchant ships taken up for conversion to bomb vessel in April 1797, all being fitted for the novel feature of low-angle fire.

Acknowledgments

THERE ARE MANY DEBTS which it is a delight to acknowledge. In the intellectual sphere, several of my colleagues at the National Maritime Museum have been of great assistance. David Lyon has been a fount of wisdom as well as a perceptive critic throughout the gestation of this work. He also read a early version of the text, providing many useful observations. Diana Cashin not only read the text and smoothed some of the bumpy passages but was also the source of some word processing wizardry, and for that much thanks. Brain Lavery supplied references and copies of papers at Shugborough, the home of Lord Anson, which proved helpful. Two former colleagues deserve mention: Ann Shirley (née Savour) brought to my attention her work on the *Racehorse* and *Carcass*, which has proved a mainstay of the section on the Arctic use of bomb vessels; and Alan Pearsall, who over the years has forgotten more on this subject than I pretend to know. At Conway, Robert Gardiner, to whose skill as an editor must be added the generosity of a fellow researcher. His references have advanced and improved this work immeasurably. Last but by no means least is Carol, who has lived with the project from the start. There can be no greater commendation. This book is dedicated to her. It only remains to say that all errors are mine and mine alone.

Preface

THE THREAD OF DEVELOPMENT which links the first of the sailing bombs in British service to the last is barely 130 years. During this period there was a slow refinement of the type. The argument which runs throughout this book is that bombs were treated as a specialist sub-type but also a part of the mainstream. They were a huge drain on the Exchequer in terms of equipping both with ordnance and men. On the other hand they were treated as disposable items either when written off after several bombardments had severely shaken them, or else left to slowly rot away at the peace. This in many ways reflects the eighteenth century way of war. Small ships could be built quickly, ordnance and people were less easily obtained. It is hoped that this book will give some insight into the Royal Navy's continued adherence to the bomb vessel as a separate type, even after the French – who originated the type – had moved away from the concept. The book deals with the large sailing bomb vessel and does not cover the many variations of mortar vessel in any depth.

Introduction

THE BOMB VESSEL WAS UNIQUE amongst the fighting vessels of the age of sail in that its primary role was not to fight other men of war. Instead its origins can be traced to the continuing conflict between Christian Europe and the Muslims.

By the seventeenth century the Ottoman Empire stretched throughout North Africa as well as deep into the Balkans; at the zenith of their expansion in 1683 the Turks had reached the gates of Vienna. The virtually autonomous Barbary States of North Africa sent their privateers – universally regarded as pirates by the Christian powers – throughout the Mediterranean and as far as the Thames estuary and Iceland.[1]

The British, Dutch and French all sent punitive expeditions against the Barbary States throughout the mid-seventeenth century. The attacks were carried out by warships carrying their artillery in what had become the conventional way, on the broadside. The guns therefore only had a limited amount of traverse and elevation. This in turn meant that against fortifications, even those in North Africa which were not as complex as in Europe, the fire of the attacking ships could only be directed in or near the horizontal plane against the curtain walls and bastions of forts. The cannon aboard ship would fire solid shot which might eventually cause a breach in the walls or other structures aimed at. However, time was needed to cause such damage, as was deliberate rather than rapid fire. This in turn would require that the firing ships be relatively stable platforms, at a constant range and with no distractions from the enemy. It was unusual for most of these preconditions to be present in such operations and consequently they were of limited effect.

The seventeenth century was a period of great advances in the science of fortification. However, running parallel with developments in fixed defences, there were counterbalancing advances in the means to prosecute sieges. One of the most important was the development of the mortar. This weapon fired either explosive shells or incendiary carcasses at an angle of 45 degrees or more, in a high arcing trajectory, so attacking in the vertical rather than the horizontal plane, and usually out-ranging conventional cannon. The combination of the explosive and the incendiary could be a powerful weapon against relatively 'soft' targets – towns, harbours, etc – as well as fortifications.

The mortar had seen service on land for two centuries, but it was only in France that there was the combination of the political will and the technological expertise to send the mortar to sea. The French king Louis

Randon engraving of a late seventeenth-century French bomb.

This contemporary engraving shows the layout of the first generation of French bomb 'galiotes'. The mortars – two abreast before the main mast – are invisible behind the weather cloths, and the defensive armament is confined to an area beneath the quarterdeck. The ship has been tentatively identified as *L'Ardente* of 1692.

XIV, as a Christian prince, felt it was an obligation to defend Christian Europe – specifically, French Mediterranean interests – against the Muslims. As the apotheosis of the seventeenth century statesman, the *Roi Soleil* wanted the propaganda advantage of defending the faith as much as the achievement of his foreign policy aims in the cockpit of Europe and on the Italian littoral. He also had in his service the foremost military engineer of his age, Sebastien Vauban, whose command of siege-craft and fortification became a byword and set the standard for the rest of Europe for a generation. It was in 1680 that the Chevalier Bernard Renau d'Elicagary, a protégé of the naval administrator Colbert, put forward the idea of sending the mortar to sea.[2]

The upshot was the ordering of five vessels called *galiotes à bombe*. The first of these was fittingly called *Bombarde* and was built at Dunkirk by Hendrik in 1681.[3]

Table 1: THE FIRST FRENCH BOMB VESSELS[4]
Specification

Armament:	Mortars		Secondary		Men
Design	2 x 12in		4 x 6pdrs		
As completed	2 x 12in		4 x 6pdrs		

	Gun deck ft-ins	Keel ft-ins	Breadth ft-ins	Depth in hold ft-ins	Burthen tons
Design	70-8		20-10		
As completed					
Bombarde	70-8		20-10		
Foudroyante	70-8		20-10		
Menaçante	70-8		20-10		
Brûlante	70-8		20-10		
Cruelle	70-8		20-10		

It is interesting to note that all five vessels of this prototype class were struck from the list of the French Royal Navy at a time when many of the capital ships of that navy were also laid up for want of funds. This perhaps reflects the fact that they were expensive to equip and send to sea, but equally that they were of limited value to a monarch who had continentalist aspirations and whose navy could not gain the command of the sea that would have allowed bomb vessels to be used against the coastlines of his principal enemies.

THE FIRST FRENCH BOMBS

As the prototypes of all bomb vessels, it is worth giving a limited description of the French vessels of this date. By a quirk of fate that may be more than coincidence, an English shipwright, Edward Dummer, was making a technical survey of Mediterranean shipping in 1683 and seems to have been present at Toulon when the French were carrying out trials of the new ship type; he recorded, and illustrated, his impressions in a manuscript book entitled *Voyage Around the Mediterranean* and now preserved in the British Library. He described the 'French galliote charged with mortar pieces' as follows:

The vessels themselves are like our ketches saving that these are square sterned; each of them are fixed with two mortar pieces ... To defend themselves from galleys they have a half deck and three good pieces of cannon on each side, and in case of other shots between wind and water there is 4 feet thickness of timber, whose heads remain bare and uncovered, evenly cut off with the deck between bulkhead and bulkhead...[5]

It is noteworthy that the hull of the vessel had to be very strong in order to absorb the recoil of very powerful weapons – comparable with the largest used in siege trains ashore to reduce fortresses – and also to take the sheer physical weight of the pieces themselves, not just to resist solid shot as Dummer suggests. To this end a vessel which had a low length-to-breadth ratio would be required, ie with a relatively short waterline length and broad in the beam. At 70ft 8in in length and with a beam of 20ft 10in these vessels had a length-to-breadth ratio of approximately 3.5 to 1. It has been argued that their hull lines were based on the mercantile galliot or hooker type, and Dummer compares them with the not dissimilar English ketch; but he stresses the square stern, and visual evidence shows little resemblance, so their designation as *galiotes à bombe* may reflect little more than the rig, which was not common in France. Whatever its origins, the hull form needed the right combination of internal capacity – to take the strengthening for the mortar beds and give space for the bomb rooms – and also to provide sufficient stability to carry a heavy load, in this case the mortars, relatively high above the waterline.

The French strengthened their vessels to carry the mortar beds by placing beams in what would have been the hold space. The first layer of reinforcing was laid fore and aft, the next transversely and thereafter alternately one way then the other until just below deck level where coiled rope was placed as a shock absorber (earth had been used at first but rope proved lighter and more resilient). Over this were laid the carlings for the mortar beds; these were nailed through the rope coils to the beams below.

The mortars, being placed in the waist of the vessels and abreast each other, were fixed to fire over the bow, described by Dummer thus:

The mortars are cast in a table of brass at an angle of the greatest random [range] and are fixed first into a six inch piece of plank and then firmly fastened between two beams starboard and larboard of the main stay, not moved by the power of firing nor by the motion of the sea.

The chambers of these mortars are not straight or cylindrical but concave and oval, and charged with loose powder and is the only reason why they have so much overshot the cannon of Algier and Genoa [another early French bombardment]. For in the material parts they differ no otherwise from mortars of ordinary use....[6]

There was no way to train the mountings except by altering the heading of the whole vessel. To be able to fire the mortars without damaging itself, the vessel could not have a mast forward of their position, and the two masts which were fitted were both rigged abaft of midships. Special arrangements had therefore to be made for the rigging of the masts. When in action the topmasts were struck down and much of the standing and running rigging also unshipped. The main stay was reinforced by being partly made of chain. Probably this was a development from the technique of slinging yards in chains when going into action in order to give extra security.

All of these unique characteristics – weight and type of ordnance, heavy recoil, rigging problems, the need for a stable platform – would remain constants throughout the history of the bomb vessel on both sides of the Channel.

Illustration from Dummer's *A Voyage in the Mediterranean*.

The main features of early French bomb vessels as investigated by Dummer (the waist bulwark is cut away to show the mortars). This manuscript report, with its accompanying illustrations, was the first British intelligence of the new weapon, and was clearly influential in the design of the first British bombs.

Part 1: Design History

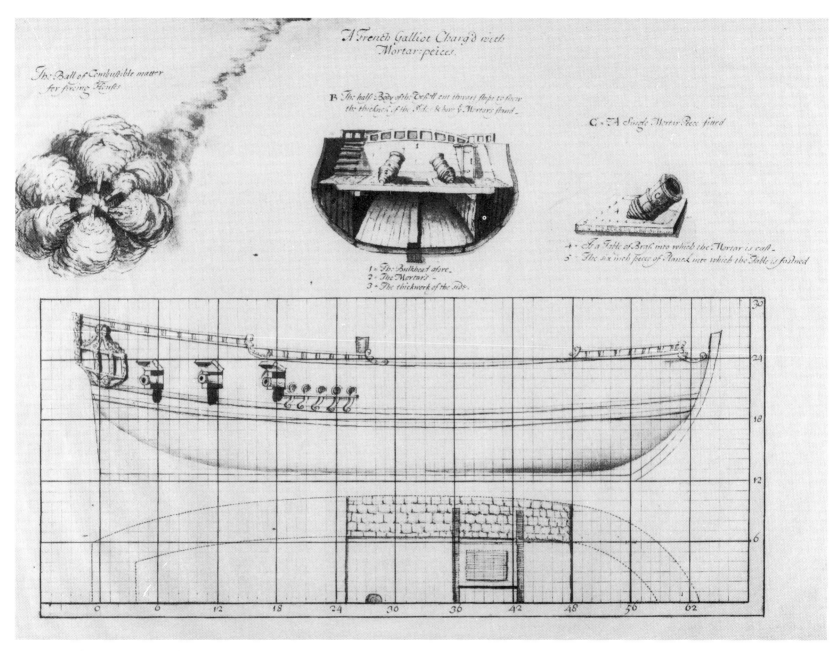

Illustration from Dummer's *A Voyage in the Mediterranean*.

Dummer's draught shows the main features of French bombs, with additional specific details such as the mortars cast integrally with their beds. The cross-section perspective is dubious, making the mortars' line of fire appear to cross the centreline but all the evidence suggests they were fired parallel with the ship's centreline.

1. The First British Bomb Vessels

THE BRITISH—OR MORE PROPERLY before the Act of Union, the English – were not long in following the French in the introduction of this new type of vessel. One authority[7] has stated that the bomb vessel, along with the fireship, were early seagoing examples of complete weapons systems, in which 'platform', equipment and operating technique combine to perform a specific mission. That mission was shore bombardment, but in British service the bomb vessel was to be used against targets across the world. Whereas in the Mediterranean the bomb saw early action against the Barbary States, in British service the targets were likely to be the ports and harbours of European powers, or their colonies. This formed an important restraint since the attitude of Western Europe's 'civilised' nations to sieges and bombardments of town and fortresses had undergone a change since the end of the Thirty Years War. The atrocities committed by succesful besiegers against garrisons and townspeople during that and earlier wars were becoming less and less acceptable as the seventeenth century changed into the eighteenth, precisely when the bomb vessel was to reach its apogee. This change in the moral climate would to some degree limit the indiscriminate use of this type of craft.

Given the highly specialised nature of the craft and their weapons, the number of accessible targets was limited in geographical terms to any coastal town, installation or fortification which could serve some strategic purpose. Within Europe the arsenal towns of an opponent were the obvious targets, as were the privateering bases for the same reason. In both cases destroying enemy vessels and dock facilities would reduce an opponent's ability to disrupt trade and challenge Britain at sea.

This in turn would presuppose that the enemy in question had either a European coastline which could be attacked by bomb vessels, or some similarly vulnerable colonial possessions as targets. In some ways it was fortuitous that the opponent Britain had faced three times in the seventeenth century was no longer the enemy but an ally: fortuitous because the numerous shoals and inlets of the Dutch coast rendered most of the towns and harbours less easily accessible to a force attacking from the sea. There is a certain historical irony in the fact that France was to be the main victim of her own invention, when adopted by the British, for France had both coastline and colonial possessions which would be vulnerable to attack by bomb vessels as soon as she lost command of the sea.

THE BRITISH PROTOTYPE BOMBS

The value of the bomb vessel in English strategy would have been immediately obvious to the Admiralty, but equally clearly it had no real peacetime role. Thus, despite the information from Dummer, the first English bomb vessel was not ordered until 1687, when James II began to fear for the security of his throne. The prototype English bomb was the *Salamander*, launched from the royal dockyard at Chatham in 1687,

and soon followed by the purpose-built *Firedrake* and the converted *Portsmouth* in 1688. The *Portsmouth* was rebuilt from a yacht originally launched in 1679. She foundered at the Nore in the Great Gale in 1703.[8]

Both the *Firedrake* and the *Portsmouth* were built at Deptford, the yard which was to have a central role in the construction and fitting of bomb vessels in the British service.

It is interesting to note that the first three vessels in British service were not built to a single draught, and indeed did not have the same dimension as each other, as did the French vessels shown in Table 1. The *Salamander* was the prototype and was followed by two heterogenous sisters, one purpose-designed and the other converted. This is not surprising given the experimental nature of the first group.

To support these vessels a small captured Fifth Rate, the *Helderenberg*, was converted to act as a tender. This established the usual mode of operating bomb vessels, whereby tenders acted as storeships for extra powder and shells and provided accommodation for the artillerymen who manned the mortars in action.

It is unlikely that these ships were entirely satisfactory, and in any case *Firedrake* and *Helderenberg* were lost early in the war that followed the replacement of James II with William III. An interim measure was the conversion in 1691 of another yacht of similar size to the *Portsmouth*, the *Kitchen* of 1670. The refitting was a major piece of work completed in July 1692, giving the ship the revised dimensions of 59ft 0in on deck, 49ft 6in keel, 19ft 6in breadth and 8ft depth in hold, for a builder's measurement of 100 tons. The ship survived active service to be sold

Table 2: THE FIRST BRITISH BOMB VESSELS
Specification

Armament:	Mortars		Secondary		Men
Design	2 x 12¼in*				
As completed	2 x 12¼in*				

	Gun deck ft-ins	Keel ft-ins	Breadth ft-ins	Depth in hold ft-ins	Burthen tons
Design		•			
As completed					
Salamander	64-4	54-6	21-6	8-4	134
Firedrake	85-9	68-0	27-0	9-10	279
Portsmouth	71-0	59-0	21-4	9-0	143

Notes: *Not certain but probable since the similar-sized *Portsmouth* managed two; either way, the calibre was probably 12¼in, which preceded the later standard 13in. Proposed defensive armament was: *Salamander* 8 minions and 2 falconets (35 men); *Firedrake* 6 minions (6ft), 2 minions (5½ft), 4 falcons (4ft), 2 brass coursier [chase] pieces (9ft); *Portsmouth* 8 minions (4½ft), 2 falcons (4ft) and 50 men. This armament seems very large and the ships may have carried fewer guns in service.[9]

Building data

Name	Ordered	Builder	Laid down	Launched	Sailed	Fitted at	Fate
Salamander				1687			BU 1703
Firedrake		Harding		1688			Captured 1689
Portsmouth				1688			Foundered 1703

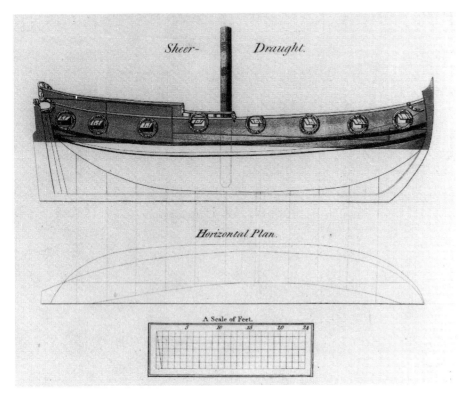

Draught of a bomb ketch from Charnock's *History of Marine Architecture*.

This drawing was tentatively identified by Dr R C Anderson as the *Salamander*, perhaps based on a now-lost draught. The absence of a mizzen probably means that it was fitted in a tabernacle and could be lowered when required. The lute stern was similar to that adopted for the 1695 ketches.

at the end of the war in 1698.

William's naval administration was inexperienced, but when applied to the novel strategic problem of a war with France, this apparent disadvantage often manifested itself as an openness to new ideas – and from some unlikely quarters. At a time when a Venetian galleass was under consideration (not very seriously, admittedly), it is hardly surprising to find the lack of native expertise in bomb design addressed by the appointment of an émigré Frenchman, Jean Fournier, as Master Builder of Bomb Vessels in 1689. According to Charles Sergison, the Clerk of the Acts between 1690 and 1719, Fournier submitted a design like the ones he had built at Toulon, although the language barrier seems to have been a great handicap in understanding the exact nature of Fournier's experience. In the event, it seems that Fournier was an artillery expert rather than a shipwright and his value was limited to advice on the fitting of the mortars. Fournier's design was regarded as suitable only for the Mediterranean:

> She hath an extreme broad floor whereby we judge she will be leewardly and a short sailer by the wind. Howsoever she may do well in case she be employed near home or in a fair weather sea, as it is commonly within the Straits [Mediterranean], but do not think her

fit for the British seas, much less for service further abroad lest for want of the good qualities of sailing and working in a sea she should lose company and want a tow.[10]

This is an early manifestation of the Royal Navy's concern for seakeeping and long-range cruising ability in its ships – even the unhandy bombs – and this requirement was to influence the next group of ships. Fisher Harding, who had built the *Firedrake*, was also consulted, and as built the next group seem to have adopted the *Firedrake*'s dimensions, and the French layout of the mortars.

THE FIRST CLASS OF BOMBS

The next group would be constructed to a common specification and, as David Lyon has pointed out, it would appear to be the beginnings of the system of building classes of vessels to a common specification, although not yet to a common design.[11]

As built they varied somewhat in dimensions, but were probably otherwise very similar. It is likely that all were ship rigged: the *Mortar* and *Serpent*, referred to as 'mortar frigates' in official correspondence[12] – certainly were, and the *Firedrake* damaged her foremast during the bombardment of Cadiz, so she cannot have been rigged as a ketch (which had no foremast). This class was much closer in design to a conventional cruiser than the experimental ships, with two continuous decks rather than the normal single upper deck, and a heavier defensive armament of eight 15cwt sakers (*c*6pdrs) on deck, four 7cwt minions (*c*4pdrs) on the quarterdeck, and six pedereroes (swivel guns) forward where there were no gunports, plus a crew of 65 men.[13] From the point of view of command, they were classed as Fifth Rates, rather than as sloops like the later bombs, a fact of great significance to Stephen Martin, who was made post in the *Mortar*, after his time as a commander in the *Blast*.[14]

In early 1693 Dummer (by now a Navy Board Officer) was seeking the most efficient rig for the new type of vessels, and he wrote on the 28 January to Harding at Deptford yard:

> If there be a foremast it must be but a small one, and so stept in a socket and fall forward as a Hoy's masts do that go through bridges. They must have a forecastle and many other contrivances, which must be informed of from the French Engineer [Fournier] who cast the mortar that will be ordered to sea in little time.[15]

From this quotation it can be seen that both the rig and other features of the British bombs were still a matter of intense debate. But what is also of note is the deference to Fournier on technical matters. This is perhaps not so surprising when it is considered that the bomb in British service was only some five years old.

In March, Dummer wrote once again, this time to Robert Lee at Chatham as well as Harding at Deptford (it would appear from the date of these letters that these exchanges refer to the 1693 group of vessels). The letter (written on 2 March 1692/3) is quoted *in extenso* as it casts light not only on Dummer's view of the bomb vessel, but also the fact that the British were looking to improve the basic type:

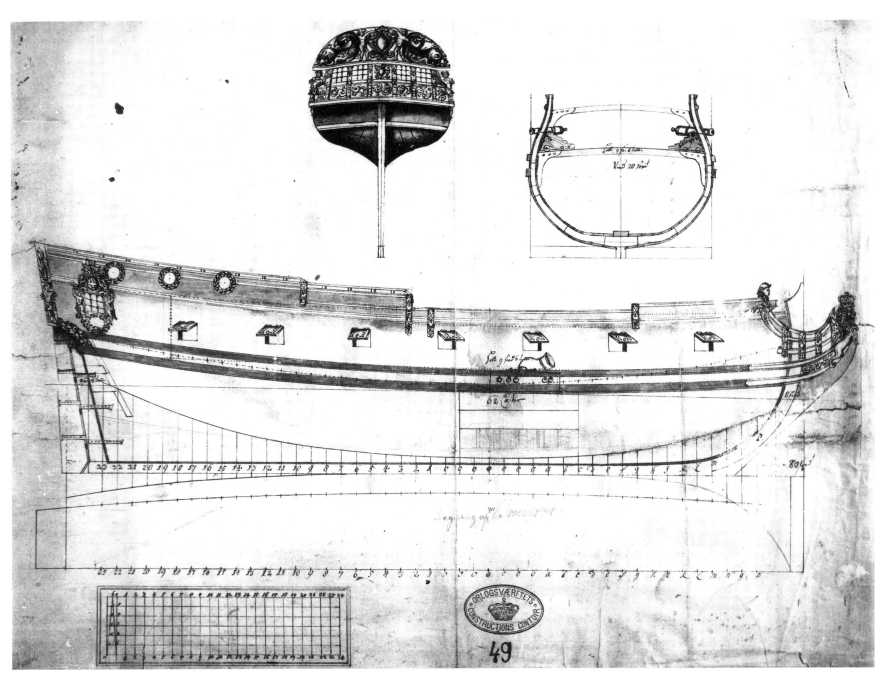

Mortar, 1693, profile, section and stern.

This is one of the few surviving plans of the early classes of bombs. The mortars would appear to be abreast, as discussed in the text. What is noticeable is the high level of stern decoration on such small and relatively expendable vessels, but perhaps commensurate with their status as Fifth Rate 'bomb frigates'. *(Rigsarkivet, Copenhagen)*

The well fixing of the new bomb vessels now building with masts and other geer proper for the use of them at sea will require a little study more than ordinary fore being above the shape of ketches whose sort of masting have suited better with the nature of such artillery which is to be fixed for shooting forward for them it would only require the casting of the main and top mast stays, but this must have a fore mast by reason of its magnitude which also must be contrived to be disposed of when the vessel comes to service. My thoughts lead me to suggest a single pole mast without topmast and topsail to step in a case above the forecastle, to strike forward upon all occasions, to have a more that ordinary hoyst of sail, to be taunt [tall] but narrow. The yard to be always struck on the crown of the course before the mast be laid forward, for working the Mortars is the manner I suppose to accomodate them to their purpose and I think a light sail ahead is more easy to ye vessel's going. Wherefore I desire your opinion with account of the dimentions you think this mast ought to be of and if you have other thoughts more advantageous to communicate them to Robert Lee at Chatham.

Dummer is still toying with the idea of a folding foremast which would lie along the bowsprit when the ship went into action. In another letter he explains how this arrangement could be made to work, with blocks and hoist on the main mast to raise and lower the foremast. It is also apparent that Dummer is aware of the problems of the ketch rig for these vessels; it has to be said that his ideas are novel, but whether they would have solved the problems of early bombs in terms of their handling under sail has to be questioned.

On the 22 March, Harding and Lee returned their views on masting the bomb vessels. They were in favour of 'masting the vessels Pink fashion',[17] *ie* three-masted. Dummer agreed with the proposal, the only problem appearing to be that Lee and Harding could not agree on the dimensions best suited, so Dummer asked for their second thoughts on the matter. The upshot of these deliberations was the 1693 class of bombs. These must be seen as very much experimental vessels, in terms of rig and hull size and form.

The first British bomb vessels had been ketch rigged, much the same as their French counterparts. Their hulls were approximately the same ratio of length to breadth and the hull form was also basically similar, except for the pink or flute stern, whereas the *Mortar* class was a clear attempt to produce a more seaworthy and ship-like bomb. Although it is by no means certain, there is evidence that all the early British bombs had two mortars mounted abreast in the waist like their French inspiration. It is quite clear that the first two groups of bomb vessels did not have their mortars placed on traversing mountings as originally built (see below); but there is firm evidence that most of them carried two mortars, so if they were mounted on the centreline they would have had to have been placed before the foremost mast (which was impossible with ship rigged vessels and, given the deck space, not much more likely with a ketch). Alternatively, they could have been set to fire at fixed angles of training on the broadside, but this seems like a wholly unnecessary complication, offering no advantage over the proven French system. Perhaps the crowning piece of evidence is the Danish draught of the *Mortar*, which shows only one mortar, and since Martin shipped two in April 1702, they can only have been fitted abreast – showing up as one on a profile draught.

The vessels of this class were much the same length as the first *Firedrake*, and although 3ft less in the beam, they were similar in tonnage. Both *Firedrake (i)* and the 1693 group had larger dimensions than was to be the case for the next group – built in 1695 – and these dimensions were not to be reached again until the *Alderney* of 1734, which with a tonnage of 262 and a length of 90ft marked the next step in the evolution of the type in the British service. It would be some sixty years before there would be a large class built to greater dimensions than those of the 1693 group.

The bomb vessel was a relatively large investment, which could produce no return when not actually employed in bombardments. As a result the Admiralty intended to use the *Mortar*s as cruisers until needed, and this may have had some bearing on their design characteristics. Even so, the Navy Board and the dockyards felt that the time and expense was not justified to produce what could only be a second class cruiser. Fournier, who was regarded as their 'designer', was brought in to give his opinion, which could be summarised under three heads:

1. It would be impossible to cut the necessary extra ports without weakening vital strength members;

2. Even removing the mortars and the forecastle would not lighten the ships much;

3. They were too heavily built ever to be good sailers.[20]

This last point was reiterated by the Commissioner of Chatham Dockyard when sending the costs for the conversion, pointing out 'I need not mention to you the hazards and inconveniences that a man of war with small force and no heels [*ie* speed] would daily be exposed to.'[21]

This was all very well, but a navy perennially short of small cruisers in wartime was unlikely to agree; indeed, throughout the remaining history of the bomb, the type was to find employment as sloops when not required for bombardment, and on occasion for a multiplicity of other minor roles.

Table 3: *FIREDRAKE* GROUP, 1693
Specification

Armament:	Mortars		Secondary		Men
Design	2 x 13in				
As completed	2 x 13in		8 sakers, 4 minions, 6 x ½pdr swivels		

	Gun deck ft-ins	Keel ft-ins	Breadth ft-ins	Depth in hold ft-ins	Burthen tons
Design	85-2½	66-0	24-1	9-10	202⁸⁶/₉₄
As completed					
Firedrake	85-2½	66-0	24-1	9-10	202⁸⁶/₉₄
Granado	87-0	73-0	26-10		279
Mortar	85-0	66-0	24-0	10-0	279
Serpent	86-0	69-9	26-6	9-9	260⁴⁶/₉₄

Building data

Name	Ordered	Builder	Launched	Fate
Firedrake		Deptford Dyd/Harding	Jun 1693	Foundered 1703
Granado		Fowler, Rotherhithe	26 Jun 1693	Blown up 1694
Mortar		Chatham Dyd/ Lee	1693	Wrecked 1703
Serpent		Chatham Dyd/ Lee	1693	Lost 1694

The Mortar Bomb Cap' Steph Martin Commander at the Taking of Eigo 12° 1702

Sketch of the *Mortar* by Captain Martin.

Martin was the commanding officer of this ship so the accuracy of the drawing (from his memoirs) cannot be doubted. It not only confirms the rig but also matches the Danish draught quite closely. It depicts the ship from two angles, as was a common convention of the maritime painting of the period, and the boat being towed astern in the quarter view is interesting given that boats were not allocated to later bombs.

A NEW DIRECTION – THE CLASS OF 1695

The new bombs went into action under Benbow in an attack on St Malo in November 1693, but their performance was far from satisfactory. A committee was set up to propose improvements (see below), and in the meantime for the 1694 season a large number of merchant ships were converted. The strategy of coastal attack, particularly on privateer bases, was kept up during 1694 and was to be further expanded in 1695 when a squadron of bombs was sent with Russell's fleet to the Mediterranean. Clearly, far larger numbers would be required for the new season, and a class of ten purpose-built bombs was planned for completion in 1695.

Table 4: THE *BLAST* CLASS, 1695
Specification

Armament:	Mortars		Secondary		Men
Design	2 x 12½in		4 x 2pdrs		30
As completed					

	Gun deck ft-ins	Keel ft-ins	Breadth ft-ins	Depth in hold ft-ins	Burthen tons
Design	66-0	50-6	23-2	10-0	143
As completed					
Blast	66-0	50-6	23-2	10-0	143
Basilisk	72-2	57-4	23-2	10-2	163¼
Carcass	66-6	50-6	23-2	10-0	143^{14}/94
Comet	66-2	50-6	23-2	10-0	144
Dreadful	66-10½	50-6	23-6	10-1	147^{23}/94
Furnace	65-6	50-6	23-4	10-0	144^{21}/94
Granado	64-5	50-6	23-8½	10-0	147^{75}/94
Serpent	65-6	49-8	23-0	10-0	139^{71}/94
Terror	65-6	50-6	23-6½	10-2	149
Thunder	65-6	50-6	23-6	10-0	147^{88}/94

Note: All ships of this class seem to have carried identical armaments.

Building data

Name	Builder	Launched	Fate
Blast	Johnson, Blackwall	1695	Yard craft 1721
Basilisk	Redding, Wapping	1695	BU 1729
Carcass	Taylor, Rotherhithe	1695	Sold 1713
Comet	Johnson, Blackwall	1695	Taken 1706
Dreadful	Graves, Limehouse	6 May 1695	Burnt 1695
Furnace	Wells, Horsleydown	18 Apr 1695	BU 1725
Granado	Castle, Deptford	1695	BU 1718
Serpent	Chatham Dyd, Lee	1695	Taken 1703
Terror	Davis, Limehouse	11 Jan 1695	Taken & blown up 1705
Thunder	Snellgrove, Limehouse	1695	Taken 1696

To meet the requirement for numbers at a time when there were many other calls on the navy's resources, the ships had to be small. In this they may have been influenced by the mercantile conversions of the previous year, but they certainly reverted to the ketch rig and the approximate dimensions of the original English bomb, the *Salamander*. However, they benefited from the first major English contribution to bomb vessel design, the traversing mounting. This allowed two mortars to be placed fore and aft on the centreline, with the ketch's main mast nearer amidships for a better balanced rig; making more economical use of the ship's length, while requiring less breadth because the mortars were no longer side by side, allowed the hull dimensions to be reduced considerably. The smaller hull inevitably compromised seagoing characteristics, and there is a temptation to see these vessels as a cheap home-waters craft for Channel employment – but the exigences of the service sent them abroad on a number of occasions.

For overseas deployment one or both of their mortars were carried by a tender. The *Blast* of this class, when sent across the Atlantic under Martin's command, transferred her forward mortar to the storeship *Suffolk Hagboat* 'according to the usual custom when they are designed for a foreign voyage, which otherwise, in the small bomb ketches, would endanger their foundering...'[22]

The return voyage was made without either mortar, the vessel surviving a storm which 'rolled her guns under' and dismasted her; Martin described the three-masted jury rig under which the voyage was completed as 'a pink coverted from a ketch', suggesting that the only difference between the two types was the rig.[23]

His drawing of the event shows two small guns per side on deck abaft the main shrouds.

Apart from the mercantile conversions, another possible influence on the design may have been contemporary man-of-war ketches employed by the navy for minor cruising duties. For example, the ketch *Hart* built at Rotherhithe and launched in 1691 had the following dimensions: length on the deck 62ft 6in, on the keel 50ft 8in, breadth 18ft 11¼in, depth 9ft 1in. The only significant difference was in the beam which, at some 4ft 3in less, was considerably narrower. The ketch *Hind* was also of similar dimensions: 63ft on the deck, 52ft 6in on the keel, a breadth of 18ft 8½in and a depth of 9ft 1in. This comparison is important as bomb vessel were 'hostilities only' craft which inevitably would see more service in auxiliary functions than in the role for which they were originally intended.

Not only were the dimensions similar to those of mercantile vessels of like tonnage, the builders of this class were in fact the merchant yards of the Thames. And, as was to be the case throughout the eighteenth century, bomb vessels were to be mostly built in the merchant yards, as were their near-cousins the sloops, brigs, fireships, and so on. This was to free the royal yards for the building of the largest warships and the fitting and repair of others. Therefore the merchant yards would tender for this type of specialist vessel in the same way as they would for all other smaller warship types. The fitting of the mortars and their beds would be done in the royal yards, by the Ordnance Board, as would other specialised fitting out.[24]

The relative economy of the new class can be demonstrated by reference to two sets of estimates extant for this period. These allow a comparison to be made between the costs of the two first full class of bomb vessels built for the service. The first estimate is for a series of bomb vessels which were to be built on the dimensions of the *Firedrake* of 1688 (outlined in Table 2). The Navy Board were asked to provide an estimate of how much it would cost to construct ten bomb vessels with these dimensions. This estimate is dated 7 November 1692. The principal costs are given in Table 5.

All the evidence supports the case that this estimate formed the basis of the construction of the four vessels of the 1693 programme of bombs, all of which were built in the royal dockyards and all with virtually the same dimensions as the *Firedrake* of 1688. Presumably either finance or building capacity could not support the whole programme, and in the

Table 5: COSTS OF THE 1693 SHIPS[25]

Vessel of the dimensions of the Firedrake

For Timber, Planks, Trenails, pitch, tar, mast, sundry material and workmanship, masts and yards	£1919
Furnishing with rigging and ground tackle sails and sea stores for the boatswain's and carpenter's store and eight months provisions of sea stores	£ 909
Total	£2828
Total for four	£11,312

Sketch of the *Blast* by Captain Martin.

Before being promoted into the *Mortar*, Martin was commander of the *Blast*, in which he experienced a dismasting. This drawing from his memoirs shows the jury rigged vessel, converted as he put it from a two-masted ketch to a three-masted pink.

end only four vessels were built. These figures allow a unit price to be compared with the next class. One ship of the 1693 class would have cost the exchequer £2828 (this would be without ordnance stores).

The next estimate is for the succeeding purpose-built class ordered in 1695. The estimate is dated 4 January 1694 and although originating from the Navy Board and apparently intended for ships to be built in the royal dockyards, it would seem to refer to the class which was eventually built in merchant yards on the Thames. Once again no contracts have survived, but the Navy Board estimate gives a fair basis for comparison. It is highly unlikely that the contract price of the merchant-built vessels would have varied greatly from that set out in the Navy Board estimate. The details of the estimate is given in Table 6 and again excludes any ordnance stores.

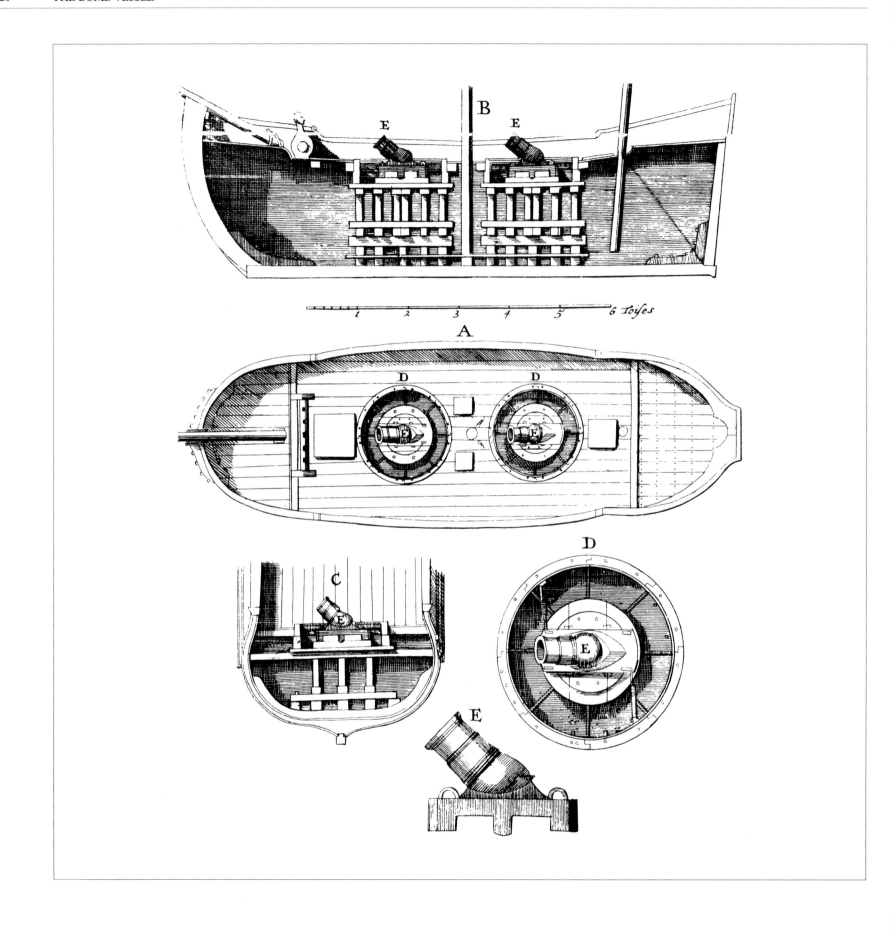

Table 6: COSTS OF THE 1695 SHIPS[26]

One bomb vessel to carry two mortars to make all proper conveniences for the sails and boatswain's and carpenter's stores

Length on deck *(ft-ins)*	65-0
by the keel *(ft-ins)*	50-6
Breadth outside *(ft-ins)*	23-0
depth of hold *(ft-ins)*	10-0
Charge for the hull, masts and planks plus the iron work and workmanship	£1469-0-0
For sail and anchor and groundtackle and all other stores, boatswain's and carpenter's	£587-0-0
Total	£2056-0-0
For nine more of the same	£18,504-0-0
Total for ten	£20,560-0-0

The ships of the 1693 class cost some £800 more than those built to the 1695 specification. This is unsurprising given that the latter were smaller by over 100 tons, construction usually being based on a price per ton.

It is interesting to compare this with a vessel designed almost ninety years later, the *Vesuvius*, proposed to be built at Woolwich in 1781.

Table 7: COST OF THE *VESUVIUS*, 1781[27]

For the hull, ironwork, ground tackle	£1467-4-6
Stores, carpenter's and boatswain's	£1090-7-10
Total cost	£2557-12-4

The price for the hull has not varied much in the intervening ninety years, whereas the price for the boatswain's and carpenter's stores has all but doubled in the same space of time. The price of the hulls could be affected positively by the relatively stable wage rates in the royal yards, given that both estimates are for vessels built in these yards.

Whilst it may come as a surprise that the price for the hulls remained stable throughout the eighteenth century, what is significant is that fact that the bomb vessel cost £2000 without the mortars and secondary armament. The price for this armament, which is discussed later in the book, would double the total cost for vessels which on average would last only two-thirds the duration of contemporary warships of the same size but different type, such as ketches and sloops. This made the bombs an expensive item to have on the establishment of the navy, although some attempt was made to recover the costs by using them in a cruising role when not required as bombs.

Draught of a bomb vessel from *Mémoires d'Artillerie*, 1698.

Because this work by Pierre Suriry de Saint Remy is French for many years the vessel was thought to be French also, despite the fact that it is radically different in many respects from the classic 'galiote'. In fact it probably represents the captured English *Thunder* and shows the main novelties of the 1695 class – the revolving mortars placed on the centreline. It also indicates the main strength members under the mortars, which developed into the shell magazines.

2. Purchased Bomb Vessels 1689-99

BOMB VESSELS WERE NOT ONLY built especially for the service but were also bought for conversion. In this they resembled their less exotic cousins, the sloops, ketches and advice boats, but their very specialised nature and cost meant that bomb vessels were not as straightforward to convert as craft used to protect convoys or carry dispatches. They were – in their prime function – the carriers of the heaviest projectiles to go to sea for nearly a century and a half, and this imposed certain restrictions. They were also a great capital investment on behalf of the government and this, if nothing else, set them apart from all other so-called minor war vessels. Nevertheless, conversions formed a large proportion of the total number of bomb vessels to see Royal Navy service.

Before looking into this it is worth pointing out that the year of the heaviest purchase of hulls for conversion to bomb vessels was 1694. This was a time when the strategy followed by William III was undergoing transformation. Britain was to keep a fleet out in the Mediterranean throughout the winter of 1694-95 and in conjunction with a change in the emphasis of the land campaign the navy was to attack coastal towns and ports. These attacks on the privateering bases in the Channel signalled an alteration in the way the war at sea had been fought thus far. This change was brought about in some measure by the decline in the fleet activities of the French navy. This was partly a reaction to the crushing defeats of Barfleur and La Hogue but was also prompted by the financial burden placed on France by the land war. Many of the larger French warships were laid up, or hired to *armateurs* – private individuals financing privateering enterprises – who fitted them out as commerce raiders.

This switch in strategy naturally provoked a change in the Royal Navy's response. This was, firstly, to provide enhanced convoy protection; secondly, the move into the Mediterranean was designed to keep the remaining parts of the French fleet bottled up in Toulon; and, thirdly, attacks were mounted on the privateering bases at Dunkirk, St Malo, and other western French ports. This last also had the objective of taking the pressure off the Allied field armies serving under William III in the Low Countries by diverting French resources into coastal defence.

As can be seen from Table 8, the price of the hull and its fitting was somewhere between £1200 and £1400, compared with £1400 for a purpose-built vessel. The conversion costs added some £450 to £500 to produce the overall cost which would total between £1800 to £1900 for hull, stores and internal fittings. This was approximately £200, or 9.5 – 10 per cent, less than for a vessel purpose built in either a merchant or royal yard.

Table 9 gives a list of vessels either brought into the service after capture or purchased from their merchant owners for use as bomb vessels.

Table 8: COSTS OF PURCHASED BOMBS, 1690-95

Name	Price of hull	Conversion	Fitting	Total
General's Adventure	£942-8-0	£583-2-11	£244-16-8	£1770-07-0
Angel	£1050-0-0	£494-6-5½	£254-11-8	£1798-18-1½
Endeavour	£444-1-2	£473-13-3	£273-11-0	£1191-05-5¾
Mary Ann	£850-0-0	£461-1-3½	£233-0-5	£1544-1-8½
Greyhound	£800-0-0	£414-2-3	£198-18-4	£1413-0-7
True Love	£725-0-0	£410-11-2	£200-17-11	£1336-9-1
Society	£650-0-0	£486-13-7	£275-12-7	£1412-6-2
Star	£789-10-0	£449-5-6	£463-5-9	£1702-1-3
Totals	£6250-19-6	£3772-16-5½	£2144-14-0½	£12,168-10-3½

Table 9: PURCHASED BOMBS, 1690-95[28]
Specification

Armament:	Mortar	Secondary			Men
Design					
As completed	1 x 13in	8 x 2pdrs*			

	Gun deck ft-ins	Keel ft-ins	Breadth ft-ins	Depth in hold ft-ins	Burthen tons
Design					
As completed					
Julian	67-0	54-2	19-0	9-4	104
Phoenix	55-0	44-10	19-2½	8-7	86
Endeavour		40-0	16-8	9-3	59
Mary Ann		44-6	18-8	10-4	82
General's Adventure		52-0	20-5	10-2	115
Society		52-0	19-1	93	102
Angel		53-0	21-3	11-0	132
Greyhound		51-0	18-8	9-1	195
Truelove		42-6	17-0	9-4	65

Notes: *The *Julian*, *Society* and *Phoenix* had 8 x 2pdrs, the *General's Adventure*, 6 x 2pdrs; the *Endeavour*, *Mary Ann*, and *True Love* had 4 minions, the *Angel* and *Greyhound* had 6 minions.

Building data

Name	Purchased	Owner	Fate
Julian	1690	Prize*	Sold 1698
Phoenix	1692		Sold 1698
Endeavour	1694		Sold 1695
Mary Ann	Apr 1694		Sold 1698
General's Adventure	1694		Sold 1698
Society	Apr 1694		Sold 1698
Angel	1694	N Smith	Sold 1696
Greyhound	1694	R Lapthorne	Sold 1698
Truelove	1694	J Gothwaite	Sold 1698

Notes: *Originally taken by the *Foresight*, and purchased into the service.

Table 10: CONVERSION COST BREAKDOWN[28]

Estimate for the conversion of the ketch Phoenix *as a bomb vessel 2nd November 1692.*

Fitting at Deptford to go to sea	£388-13
To the owner	£440
Make her fit for the West Indies	£124-7-8
For loss of freight to owner	£200
Total	£1153-0-0

These three tables make it possible to compare the cost for purchased and purpose-designed vessels and allows an estimate to be made of the financial investment, purely in terms of the ships themselves, made by the Admiralty in this type of vessel.

The vessel listed in Table 9 as *General's Adventure* would appear to be the same as that listed as *Owner's Advent* by other sources. If this is the case, then there is an almost complete listing of the cost to the Exchequer of these vessels, the only exception being the *Julian*, for which no costings could be found. Apart from the aggregated cost for the hulls, conversion and fitting which are given in Table 8, the variation in total cost of the eight vessels is given in Table 11. The figures are rounded up to the nearest whole pounds.

Table 11: COST COMPARISONS BETWEEN CONVERTED AND PURPOSE-BUILT BOMB VESSELS[29]

Vessel's name	Total cost	Average cost of purpose-built vessels
General's Adventure	£1770	
Angell	£1798	1693 class £2828
Endeavour	£1190	class of four total £11,312
Mary Anne	£1544	
Greyhound	£1412	1695 class £2056
Phoenix	£1153	class of ten total £20,560
True Love	£1335	
Society	£1411	
Star	£1702	
TOTALS	£13,315	£31,872

From the figures set out in Table 11 it is quite clear that it cost just over twice as much to build from new the two classes of 1693 and 1695, which totalled fourteen vessels, as it did to acquire, convert and fit out the nine vessels purchased in 1694. Also apparent is the great disparity in the price of the individual hulls, etc for the purchased vessels, running from a little over £1190 to nearly £1702. This would in part reflect the condition of the vessel when surveyed at Deptford as well as purchase price (which would be calculated on a standard rate for a given tonnage). Unfortunately, the author has not found any relevant surveys, so it is not possible to gain an idea of the condition or age of the vessels taken up for conversion, although the wide variation in the price of conversion and fitting out may give some indication of this.

The total investment in purchasing the hulls and fitting them out for the prosecution of the new strategy was £45,187 over the three-year period 1692-95. In terms of ships of the line this sum is approximately

Bombardment of Dieppe, 1694, contemporary engraving.

The dedication of this picture is to the Master General of the Ordnance, the Earl of Romney, while the caption mentions the 'bomb ships invented by Colonel Richards' – the man who developed the trainable mounting for mortars. This scene shows one of the classic seventeenth-century bombardments, at a period when bomb vessels were used in large numbers. If the view is accurate then many of those vessels rushed into service, including the mercantile purchases, are present here.

the price of two Third Rates without their sea or ordnance stores. The question has to be asked whether or not this was a sound investment in terms of the period of time over which the vessels would perform their prime function as opposed to that spent in secondary tasks acting as sloops, etc.

Some authorities have sought to explain the need to buy rather than build bomb vessels in this period as due to the lack of money and building capacity (especially in the royal yards).[30]

It is true (particularly for 1694-95), that a large number of Fourth and Fifth Rates were being constructed at this period, as a response to the pressure on British commerce that the French privateers were exerting; therefore both the state and the private yards were busy. In terms of finance, as a later chapter will show, the whole cost to the exchequer was not just in the hulls themselves but also in the ordnance which they carried; this could double the price as a whole.

Although the purchase of vessels from the merchant fleet may have been marginally cheaper (as we have seen) than building in the royal yards, the primary reason for purchasing rather than building was the

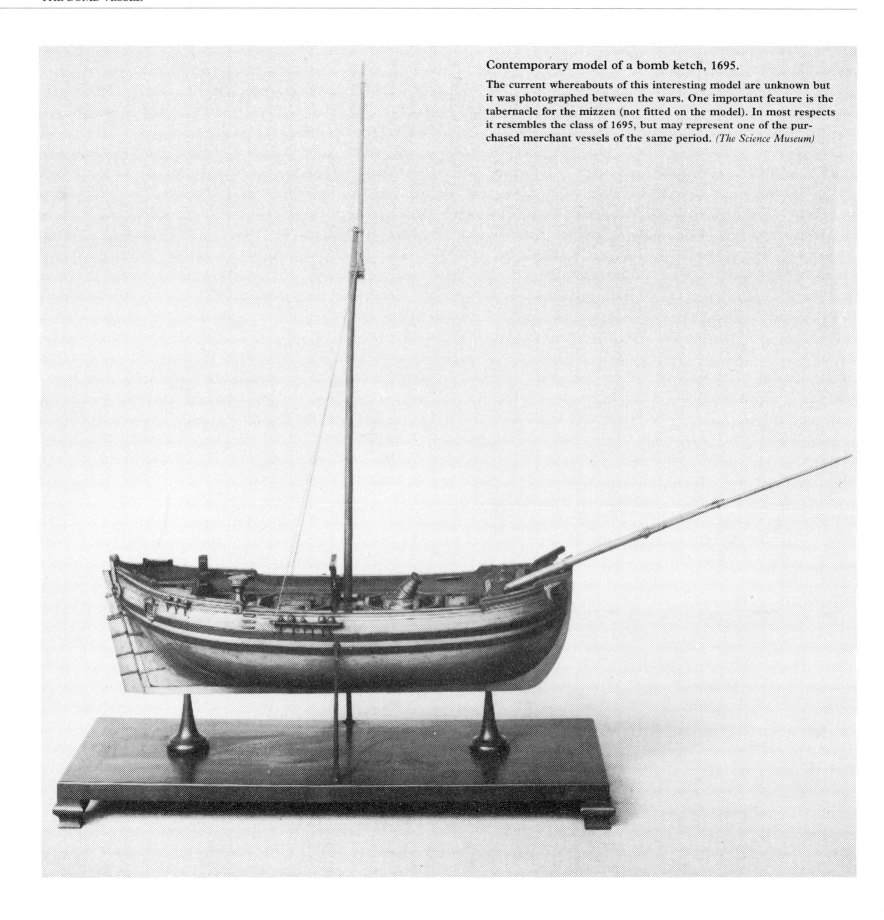

Contemporary model of a bomb ketch, 1695.

The current whereabouts of this interesting model are unknown but it was photographed between the wars. One important feature is the tabernacle for the mizzen (not fitted on the model). In most respects it resembles the class of 1695, but may represent one of the purchased merchant vessels of the same period. *(The Science Museum)*

need for rapid entry into service. The new strategy meant that the navy required specialised bomb vessels to play a part in operations planned for the campaign season of 1694. The Admiralty request for more bombs appears to originate on 2 March 1694.[31]

On that date a letter was received by the Board of Ordnance asking them to find twelve vessels for conversion to bombs. Colonel Richards, an officer of the Ordnance, was detailed to survey the shipping in the Thames to find suitable vessels. The search did not prove easy,[32] and this casts a light on the division of responsibility at this early stage in the bomb vessel's development.

Colonel Richards was instructed to look for likely vessels on the same day that the Admiralty letter was received. This he had done by about 10 March, but he had no authority to embargo the vessels from sailing and had to apply to the Admiralty for a warrant. By the time, two days later, that the Admiralty had issued the warrant (12 March), six of the vessels originally surveyed had sailed. This incident highlights the fact that owners were not all that keen to have their vessels purchased for the service at a time when there were good freight rates to be had. The six finally embargoed were ready for fitting out at Deptford by 17 March, which promoted a further exchange of correspondence between the Ordnance and the Admiralty. To make up the number the *Julian Prize*[33] was ordered to be fitted as a bomb at Chatham. On 5 April there was still not the required total of twelve vessels, as 'The owners [are] not willing to part with them'.[34]

It would not be until 26 May that some of the bomb vessels were ready to drop down to the Nore from Deptford – at one point the Ordnance Board had to request that the yard's carpenters assist their own men in the hopes of expediting the fitting out. However two of the purchased bombs (*True Love* and *Endeavour*) were not to be ready for service until August of 1694 due to there being no mortars available.

There was a series of overlapping areas which this particular incident highlights. Whilst the Admiralty sent the request for the bombs to be fitted or purchased, it was the Master General of the Ordnance who advised the King on the availability of bomb vessels, not the Admiralty.[35]

It was a responsibility of the Ordnance officers to survey the bombs already in service and also to find new vessels to fill the shortfall from the ranks of merchant vessels. The Navy Board had to survey, convert and to provide iron work and ship fittings (*eg* anchors, sails, etc) for the bombs at Deptford or Chatham, but it was for the Ordnance to provide the mortars and shells and to fit the supporting structures and facilities. It was also for the Ordnance Board to find and hire tenders for the bombs. As noted above this meant the Ordnance's carpenters would be aboard the bombs whilst they were at Deptford, working alongside the Navy Board carpenters who were also fitting them out.

Thus there was a division of responsibility at the level of grand strategy, at the executive and also on the operational level regarding bomb vessels. This could, and did, cause problems both in provision and operation of bomb vessels. What is certain is that, at this period at least, the Board of Ordnance had as much if not more control over the use and provision of bomb vessels in British service as the Admiralty.

3. Bomb Vessels 1700-39

THE YEARS FROM 1693 TO 1697 were the high water mark of the bomb vessel. More ships were employed, and a greater proportion of the national war effort was expended on them, than at any time following. The bomb vessel represented the latest technology, and as so often with these 'secret weapons' much was expected of them. Their development obviously coincided with a strategy that could make full use of them, but it is a moot point whether their existence actually inspired that strategy or merely made it more plausible. In the event, very little damage was inflicted in relation to the resources expended and the tangible results of the coastal bombardment strategy must have been something of a disappointment.

After the Peace of Ryswick there was only a short period without hostilities whilst the main protagonists drew breath. In the interval the bomb vessels which had survived the war were laid up and their mortars landed. When hostilities were renewed it was over the accession of Louis XIV's grandson to the throne of Spain in contravention of the terms of the partition treaty between William III and his allies and Louis XIV. The threat of a Bourbon-dominated Spain and her possessions in Italy was too much for the allies, who declared war in 1702.

Of the vessels built or purchased in the previously war only the following were still in service at the outset of hostilities.

Table 12: SURVIVING BOMB VESSELS IN 1702

Name	When built	Fate
Portsmouth	1679	27 Nov 1703 foundered in the Great Gale whilst at the Nore.
Firedrake	1693	Foundered 2 Dec 1703
Mortar	1693	Wrecked 1703
Blast	1695	Yard craft 1721
Basilisk	1695	BU 1729
Carcass	1695	Sold 1713
Comet	1695	Taken 1706
Furnace	1695	BU 1725
Granado	1695	BU 1718
Serpent	1695	Taken 1703
Terror	1696	Taken and blown up 1706

The only accession to frontline strength at this time was the rebuilding at Woolwich in 1703 of the *Salamander* of 1689 to the dimensions, and presumably the layout, of the 1695 *Blast* class. The details are given in Table 13.

None of the vessels which had been purchased for conversion to bomb vessels in the previous war survived into the next. Most of them were sold out of the service as soon as the war was over. Of the ten vessels still in service at the start of the war, three were lost in the first year to natural hazards and one was taken by the enemy.

The use of bomb vessels in the War of the Spanish Succession was

Table 13: *SALAMANDER*, 1703
Specification

Armament:	Mortars			Secondary		Men
Design	2 x 13in					
As completed	2 x 13in					30

	Gun deck ft-ins	Keel ft-ins	Breadth ft-ins	Depth in hold ft-ins	Burthen tons
Design	66-0	51-4	21-2	8-8½	122
As completed					
Salamander	66-0	51-4	21-2	8-8½	122

Building data

Name	Builder	Launched	Fate
Salamander	Woolwich Dyd, Lee	1703	Sold 1713

on a much reduced scale compared with that of the previous war. This is reflected in the fact that no entirely new bomb vessels were built as such during the period. The campaigns of Marlborough in Flanders and on the Rhine[36] did not call for the diversions to draw off French forces by descents on the coast. Against the privateering activities of the French the allied fleet of Great Britain and the Netherlands operated cruisers and convoys to counter the threat they posed. In fact these measures were not wholly effective and a new cruisers and convoy act was passed in 1708.[37]

Bomb vessels did see action, but not in the same numbers as between 1692 and 1697 – often only in twos or threes rather than fives or tens. In May 1702, at the outbreak of the war, there were ten bomb vessels in commission, split between eight at home and two in the squadron serving with Admiral Benbow in the West Indies. This meant that all available bomb vessels were commissioned at the start of the conflict. In August 1704, well into the campaign season, only two bomb vessels were in commission and these were seeing service in the Mediterranean. Three years later, in August 1707, three bomb vessels were in commission once again in the Mediterranean and the start of the next year, February 1708, saw three bomb vessels still in commission in the Mediterranean.[38]

The numbers of vessels in commission during the War of Spanish Succession was relatively small, the first flush of enthusiasm for the new 'terror weapon' having passed with their disappointing achievements in the previous conflict. This period should be seen as a time of technical consolidation, a period when the use of the bomb vessel was being refined, but also a time when expectations were becoming more realistic. As the lists of vessels in commission suggest, their main theatre was the Mediterranean and in operations off the Iberian peninsular. This reflected the fact that the Royal Navy's strategic horizons had been expanded since the previous war. The Mediterranean was to become a near-permanent theatre of war for all the following conflicts in what

has been called the second hundred years' war between Britain and France.

The shift in the theatre of operations from the relative proximity of the French Atlantic coast to the Mediterranean must have posed problems for those who had to serve aboard the bomb vessels. Although weather conditions may have been generally better in the middle sea, there was still the problem of the long passage to and from the station, not to mention long periods cruising with the fleet. Designed to accommodate one or two large mortars on the upper deck, most bombs had no continuous deck below the upper deck, the hold space being filled with the massive mortar beds, bomb rooms and pillars. This severely restricted the amount of space below decks given over to both officers and men, as well as for stowage for water and victuals. Whilst the problem of small vessels such as sloops and ketches operating at long distance from home was not unique to the bomb, it must have been exacerbated for these vessels precisely because of the internal design and the needs of the mortars, around which all else, including the crew, was fitted.

It is unfortunate for the historian that at this period there are no sailing quality reports, nor did any of this generation of bomb vessel serve long enough to be reported on. It is a pity because it would be interesting to know what characteristics under sail the following designs sought either to perpetuate or conversely to eliminate. As it is, no such objective judgement can be made. However, the operations which were carried out in the Mediterranean give some clues as to how these vessels handled. At the siege of Barcelona in 1705 five British bombs were involved.[39]

The *Basilisk*, Captain Blowers, was ordered to commence operations on 5 September:

2 pm. Unmoored to bomb the town. Then we fired till afternoon, 14 shells. Then Stafford Fairbourne ordered me leave off. I weighed sailed off.[40]

7th. Last night weighed to go in again and went near the town and fired 20 shells. We set fire two places. At seven, pm, weighed and went in again; and nine, anchored near the town in twelve fathoms water and fired 20 shells and 2 carcasses: and at morning weighed and came off again.

8th. Last night, the current running too strong, that we could not get in to do any good, forced to lie still.[41]

The *modus operandi* of the bomb vessels was to sail into action then moor up at predetermined points to carry out their allotted tasks. However this left them at the mercy of the wind and weather, or more so than their larger cousins. As far as can be ascertained there was no provision for the regular stowing of ship's boats on these, or later bombs, although Captain Martin's sketch of the *Mortar* at sea shows a pinnace being towed. However, in most accounts of actions one reads of small frigates or sloops supporting the bombs, so if becalmed or damaged aloft in mast and rigging they were presumably towed; they may also have been brought into or out of action with the help of support craft. Being moored up to fire also had the drawback of being a stationary target for

Sea service mortar, 1726.

The major step forward of the early eighteenth century was the development of the 'trabucco' mortar, which had trunnions cast at the base, allowing it to be elevated. This had the dual benefits of permitting the range to be adjusted by elevation, and when not in action the piece could be stowed horizontally. The draught of the *Granado* shows just such a disposition. This mortar, now preserved in the Tower of London, may be the prototype for the elevating type. *(The Tower Armouries)*

any batteries the enemy might have in range, in the same way that their land equivalents came under counter-battery fire from besieged forts.

There is some support for the view that bomb vessels of this period needed a very calm sea and fair weather; certainly, rolling and pitching cannot have enhanced accurate fire. Both at Barcelona in 1705, and Toulon in 1707, reference is made in officer reports to the need for a smooth sea before bringing the bombs into action. At the latter joint operation the bombardment of the arsenal was delayed because 'the wind blew so hard that the ships could not get in'.[42]

Thus the lack of ship's boats, and hence dependancy on other vessels to help them into and out of action, was more significant than at first it might seem. The ketch rig with the mast set so far aft may have also caused problems when it was necessary to manoeuvre close inshore to a precise position, although there is no direct evidence to support this impression.

If the hull forms and overall dimensions of the vessels did not change,

their use in action was being refined. There is some evidence that the mortars were still causing problems either through cracking or, as one contemporary put it, melting – bronze ordnance tended to go out of shape rather than break up when over-fired.[43] This particular case would appear to have been caused by a fault in casting, which is not surprising when it is considered that mortars weighed between four and five tons, and were cast in one piece. However, it was not just the size of the casting that was the problem: it was also the material, bronze. As late as 1811 brass siege pieces were withdrawn from land service as they suffered from muzzle droop if subjected to prolonged firing.

Prior to their withdrawal in the Peninsular War after 1809 the land service mortar was restricted to discharging 128 rounds in any 24-hour period, although it is not clear if the same restriction applied to sea service weapons. During the War of the Spanish Succession it is possible to quantify the number of rounds expended by vessels in some actions. On one day during the siege of Barcelona, 15 September 1705, the *Furnace* fired off 50 rounds, the *Comet* 42 and the *Carcass* 40. Over the period 4-22 September the *Basilisk* fired a total of 93 rounds, predominately shell, to the proportion of 89 shells to 4 carcasses.[44] In all over 876 rounds were fired at Barcelona by the British and Dutch bomb vessels.[45] At Toulon in 1707 the *Blast*, *Basilisk* and *Granado* are said to have fired off the best part of 100 rounds each.

This was a relatively small number, representing approximately a third of the provision for each bomb vessel at Toulon, and the damage done to the enemy was comparatively slight. The bombs set on fire *Le Sage* (58) and *Le Fortune* (52), which had been left afloat, whereas other vessels at Toulon had been deliberately scuttled by the French to avoid being badly damaged by any bombardment. The scuttled *Le Diamant* had her upperworks burnt and two smaller vessels described as frigates, *L'Andromède* and *La Salamandre*, were also damaged by shells. However, the French raised batteries ashore which drove the bombs out of range

and illustrates their vulnerability to counter fire from shore. George Byng, later to lead the British Mediterranean fleet to its crushing victory at Cape Passaro in 1718, commanded the bomb vessels on that day and highlighted the problem: 'I would we had more time but they brought guns to the water side and mauled our bomb vessels.'[46]

In 1706 two bomb vessels took part in the bombardment of Ostend, one of the principal privateering bases on the Channel coast. The vessels, the *Salamander* and *Blast*, expended the following number of rounds: *Salamander* 229 shells and 5 carcasses, the *Blast*, 192 shells and 8 carcasses.[47]

From the above it can be calculated that on average a mortar could be discharged every six or seven minutes and that bombardments were a series of staccato affairs with bomb vessels moving in and out of action rather than firing from one position in a sustained manner and then retiring from the fray. Prolonged firing almost always produced some strains on the hull and often the rigging, which could mean that they were not available all of the time and in a like manner there is at least anecdotal evidence that the mortars themselves did not always stand the strain of prolonged firings.

By the end of this war the pattern of use was set. The three actions described above had all of the ingredients which were to become associated with the employment of bomb vessels: they were joint expeditions, either in co-operation with troops already on shore, as at Ostend and Toulon, or in support of troops landed for a specific purpose, as at Barcelona. The problems of the bomb were also manifest in these actions. They could not operate on their own as they needed fleet support both for protection whilst in action and also on a number of occasions in order to bring them into or out of action by towing, using either small cruisers or their boats. There is also evidence that at this period there was some trouble with the mortars, which failed under continuous use. The bombs were also far from suitable for making long passages, and as an example of this there is reference to two of the brass mortars being sent home in the First Rate *Barfleur* in December 1705 rather than being left aboard the bomb on her homeward journey.[48]

THE LONG PEACE, 1711-39

Bomb vessels were usually laid up in peacetime, but despite the decades between 1711 and 1739 being for Britain the longest period in the eighteenth century without a major war, the story of the bomb does not come to a complete halt. In fact it was during this long peace that the the next significant step in the evolution of the bomb was taken.

Despite the pacific policy of Walpole and his ministry, throughout the period there was a series of mobilisations and near-ruptures with the continental powers, conflict with Spain and a major commitment to protecting British interests in the Baltic. This meant that a proportion of the fleet was nearly always on service either in the Mediterranean or the Baltic, although the one type of vessel missing from these armaments was usually the bomb. The period from 1711 to 1729 was certainly fallow as far as construction of new vessels was concerned, although one bomb was added to the list by capture after Admiral George Byng's

Table 14: VESSELS CAPTURED OR BOUGHT INTO THE SERVICE 1711-39

Specification

Armament:	Mortars		Secondary		Men	
Design						
As completed						
Speedwell	2 x 13in ?		?			
Thunder	2 x 13in?		6 x 6pdr		40	

	Gun deck ft-ins	Keel ft-ins	Breadth ft-ins	Depth in hold ft-ins	Burthen tons
Design					
As completed					
Speedwell	95-9½	78-9¾	25-6½	11-6	273⁶⁰/₉₄
Thunder	82-0	63-5½	27-5	10-7½	253⁶⁰/₉₄

Building data

Name	Ordered	Builder	Laid down	Launched	Sailed	Fitted at	Fate
Speedwell★	16 Nov 1715	Deptford Dyd, Stacy		27 Mar 1716			Wrecked 1720
Thunder†							BU 1734

Notes: ★*Speedwell* converted from Sixth Rate;

†*Thunder* one of the vessels captured by Admiral Byng in 1718 at Cape Passaro.

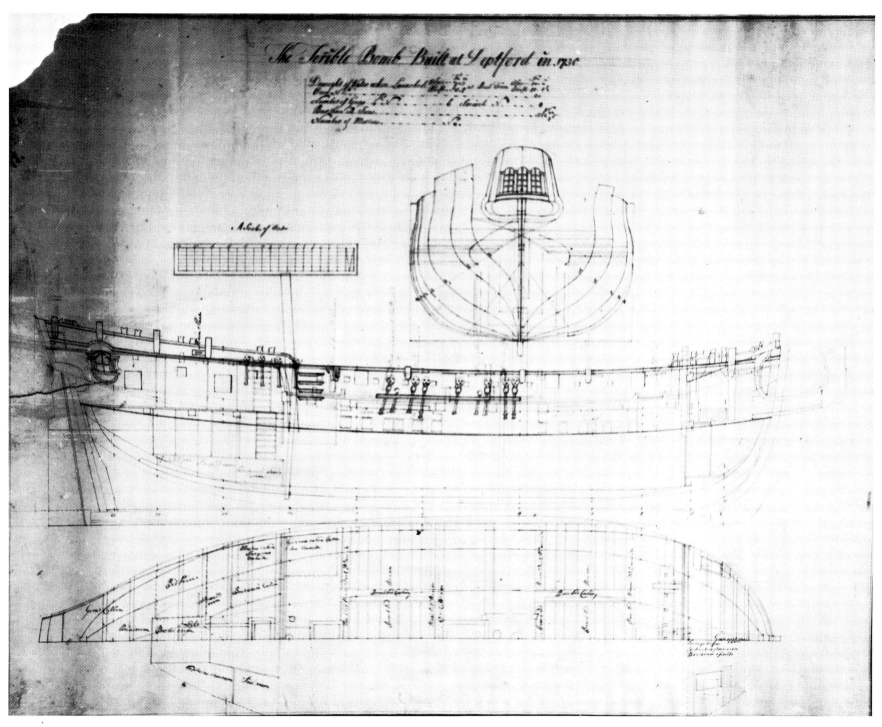

Terrible, 1730, as fitted sheer, half breadth, and body plan, taken off at Portsmouth in 1732.

This Danish draught depicts the first class to carry the new elevating mortars, although it is not apparent from the draught. Compared with the 1695 ketches, the vessel has become more warship-like, with regular rows of gunports and a quarter badge; it also has a proper stepped mizzen. *(Rigsarkivet, Copenhagen)*

victory over the Spanish off Cape Passaro in 1718.

The revival of interest in these vessels in the period around 1730 is not surprising. In 1728 Britain had nearly gone to war with Spain, and one of the chief areas of contention, after the West Indies and South America, was Gibraltar. The Spanish were keen to retake possession of the Rock, and a state of almost perpetual siege obtained on the peninsula which connected Gibraltar to the mainland. The fleet could – and did, as at Cape Passaro – impose itself on the Spanish fleet, but was less effective against the siege mortars and batteries facing the British garrison. For this a bomb vessel was ideal.

The first new bomb vessels built for the service since the *Salamander* in 1703 were to be close in terms of dimensions and the lead vessel was to carry the same name. There were to be just two vessels, both of them built in the royal dockyards at Woolwich and Deptford:

Table 15: *SALAMANDER* CLASS, 1730
Specification

Armament:	Mortars		Secondary		Men
Design	1 x 13in, 1 x 10in		8 x 4pdr, 14 swivels		60
As completed	1 x 13in, 1 x 10in		8 x 4pdr, 14 swivels		

	Gun deck ft-ins	Keel ft-ins	Breadth ft-ins	Depth in hold ft-ins	Burthen tons
Design	83-0	65-4	27-6	11-0	262⁷⁶/₉₄
As completed					
Salamander	83-10	65-5	27-7	11-1	265⁷⁶/₉₄
Terrible	83-0	65-4	27-6	11-0	262⁷⁶/₉₄

Building data

Name	Builder	Launched	Fate
*Salamander**	Woolwich DY	7 Jul 1730	Sold 1744
Terrible	Deptford DY	4 Aug 1730	Sold 1749

*Notes: *Salamander was rated as a sloop between 1730 and 1735.*

These new vessels were not a lot larger than the 1693 ships, although there was a significant addition to the breadth. In profile the hull resembled contemporary sloops, although the bombs had a fuller section and were much broader. At this time when, despite the tensions, there was no major shooting war, it seems that for the Admiralty and Navy Board the secondary cruising role of the bombs was a greater design priority than it had been with the 1695 ships. There is evidence for this in the increase in the secondary armament and the rating of the *Salamander* as a sloop for the first five years after her launch. There was a perennial shortage of small craft both in times of peace and war, and one authority has calculated that the average small vessel had life expectancy of only fourteen years.[49]

Given this relatively short life, and the absence of a peacetime need for shore bombardment, it is not surprising that attempts should have been made to suit bomb vessels for a dual function. It is perhaps pure coincidence that the *Salamander* lasted exactly the average fourteen years before being sold out of the service in 1744; the *Terrible*, however, survived until the end of the war, being sold in 1749.

These two vessels make an interesting comparison with their near-contemporay cousins of the *Cruiser* group of sloops, whose principal dimensions were as follows:

Table 16: *CRUISER* GROUP SLOOPS

	Gun deck ft-ins	Keel ft-ins	Breadth ft-ins	Depth in hold ft-ins	Burthen tons
Design	84-0	71-1	23-0	9-0	200

The gun armament is virtually the same as for the *Terrible*, which suggests that the bombs could only carry eight guns when employed as sloops. Indeed, the Danish draught of that bomb, which is clearly an 'as fitted' plan, quotes six 4pdrs and eight swivels. The difference between the rated number of crew is also a clue to employment. The *Cruiser* group were established with 80 men and the 1730 bombs with 60. By 1740 there were two manning establishments published for bomb vessels, one when fitted as a bomb and the other as a sloop, which invariably was the higher by some 25 per cent. In the case of one later class, built in 1741, as a sloop they carried upwards of a third more than as a bomb.[50]

The vessels of the 1730 group showed an increase in overall dimensions and hence in their capacity to carry a larger, and more useful, secondary armament. However, they also introduced a major innovation in armament, in the trunnioned mortar. Traversing mountings were developed for the 1695 vessels, but they were still of fixed elevation. This entailed varying the powder charge to change the range; the weight of these mortars so high in the ship also made it prudent to take them out of the bombs when on passage. A further drawback was the difficulty of covering mortars against the weather. All these shortcomings were obviated by casting mortars with trunnions at the breech end – the so-called 'trabucco' mortar – whose elevation could be varied in action, and which could be stowed flat when not in use, improving the ship's stability, and simplifying the provision of hatch covers.

There is a surviving example of a bronze 13in sea service mortar of this description known to have been cast in 1726.[51] It is the earliest recorded example of a sea service 'trabucco' and may have been the prototype. Certainly, *Terrible* and *Salamander* were the first bombs to be fitted for this species of ordnance, and the dates fit well with experiments that may be assumed to have followed the casting of the 1726 mortar. Another innovation may have been the introduction of two calibres of mortar, a 13in and a 10in, the smaller calibre being usually reserved for the after position, which was more heavily masked by rigging. Most evidence suggests that earlier bombs carried two of the same calibre – initially 12¼in and then 13in – but there are references to 10in weapons in the 1690s. However, in August 1738 these vessels carried a 13in mortar and a 10in howitzer, a mortar-like gun but one with its trunnions nearer the centre of the barrel;[52] this latter may have been substituted for a mortar at other times in their careers. The standard fit of later bombs was one each of 13in and 10in mortars, and the *Terrible* and *Salamander* were clearly a step in this direction.

The next design followed four years later and was the progenitor of

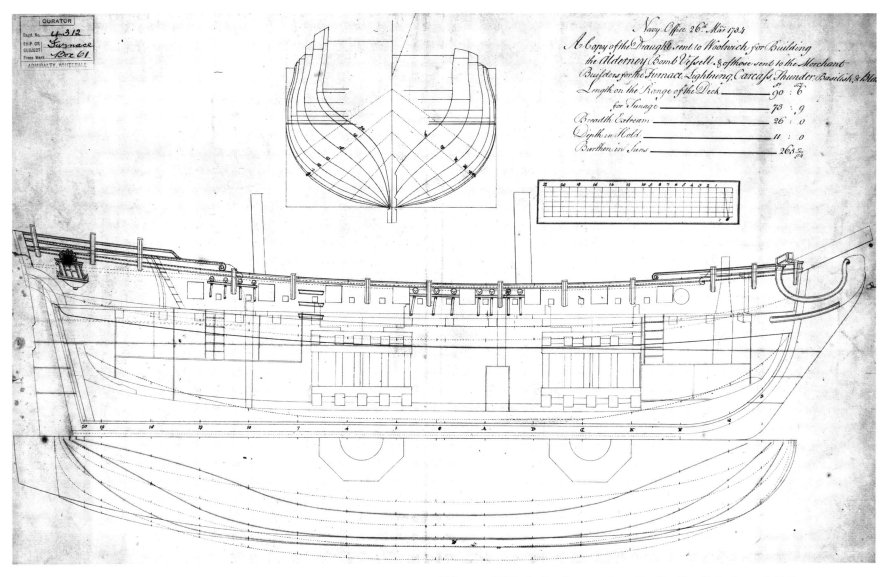

Navy Office 26th Mar 1734

A Copy of the Draught sent to Woolwich for Building
the Alderney Bomb Vessell. & of those sent to the Merchant
Builders for the Furnace, Lightning, Carcass, Thunder, Basilisk, & Bla...

Length on the Range of the Deck _____ 90 : 6
    for Tunage _____ 73 : 9
Breadth Extream _____ 26 : 0
Depth in Hold _____ 11 : 0
Burthen in Tuns _____ 265 ½/94

Alderney, 1734, design lines and profile for *Basilisk* class of 1740.

a whole series of vessels. The original draught was a piece of royal innovation, having been designed by HRH the Duke of Cumberland. Cumberland was no stranger to military matters as his involvement in the War of Austrian Succession and the suppression of the Jacobite uprising was to demonstrate. However, he is not that closely associated with the Royal Navy of the period, although as a future field officer the use of siege weapons could not have been unknown to him. His intervention also followed in a long tradition of aristocratic amateur projects put forward for naval service.

The new vessel was registered as the *Alderney* and was longer, narrower and of sharper section than her predecessors, presumably with the intention of improving her qualities under sail. It is perhaps significant that the ship was not christened with one of the traditional 'explosive' names, but was given the kind of name usually reserved for small cruisers.

Like the *Salamander* of the previous class the *Alderney* spent the first

The *Alderney* was the progenitor of the whole of the 1740s building programme – the draught clearly mentions the six *Basilisk* class bombs built in the merchant yards. The position of the mortar beds precluded a continuous deck below the upper. The fore mast is approximately a third of the way back from the beakhead and the mizzen is just before the break of the poop. This gives much more balance to the rig although it does not seem to have cured the handling problems quoted in the sailing reports for bombs built to her lines.

five years of her service rated as a sloop, which highlights the point made earlier about the desperate shortage of small cruisers for the multitude of duties required even when the navy was nominally on its peacetime establishment.

Although bombs and sloops were subject to a parallel development, the *Alderney* was a significant advance in size. By comparison, the *Drake* group of sloops built from 1740 were some 5ft less in length on the deck,

Table 17: *ALDERNEY*, 1734
Specification

Armament:	Mortars	Secondary			Men
Design	1 x 13in, 1 x 10in	10 x 4pdr, 14 swivels			60
As completed					
Alderney	1 x 13in, 1 x 10in	10 x 4pdrs, 14 swivels*			60

	Gun deck ft-ins	Keel ft-ins	Breadth ft-ins	Depth in hold ft-ins	Burthen tons
Design	90-6	72-10	26-1	11-0	262
As completed					
Alderney	90-6	72-10	26-1	11-0	262

Note: *The swivels were ½pdrs

Building data

Name	Ordered	Builder	Laid down	Launched	Fate
Alderney	27 Mar 1734	Woolwich Dyd, Hayward	1 Apr 1734	29 Mar 1734	Hulked Jamaica 1742

about 3ft less in the beam, and 2ft less in the hold. It was only towards the middle 1740s that sloops were allowed the same increase in dimensions. The draughts of the *Alderney* show the vessel pierced with eight ports well spaced out along the upper deck. Given the placement of the mortar beds, it is highly unlikely that the defensive carriage guns in the ports adjacent to the beds themselves would have been mounted when they were fitted as bombs, which would leave them, per side, two mounted amidships and two mounted under the poop.

The draughts show that the stepping of the masts was not as unbalanced as contemporary illustrations would suggest was the case with the earlier bombs. In fact the main mast was positioned just aft of the fore mortar bed, with the mizzen stepped just before the break in the poop. There was little latitude in the placement of the channels; for the main mast almost amidships and for the mizzen just on the break of the poop. However, even with the mortars on turntables, the siting of the main channels meant that the shrouds must have restricted the arc of fire of the aft mortar bed by quite some degree.

Alderney was effectively the prototype of the major bomb vessel building programme of the 1740s. Bombs built to her lines are the first for which there are sailing quality reports, which along with other material gives some indication of the state of bomb design a half-century since their introduction into Royal Navy service.

4. The War of 1739-48

THE OUTBREAK OF WAR WITH Spain occasioned by the famous severed ear of Captain Jenkins was greeted with some enthusiasm by the British trading community, which foresaw the abolition of Spanish commercial monopolies in the New World. This was to be achieved by attacks on Spanish colonies in the Caribbean and South America, a strategy in which the bomb vessel could prove most useful. In 1740 a class of six were ordered to the latest existing design, the *Alderney*. The dimensions were very marginally different but this probably represents no more than minor changes to the internal arrangements – principally that the earlier ship's flush main deck was replaced by a step down, or 'fall', aft, which gave the main cabin more headroom while reducing the topside height of the small quarterdeck that formed its roof.

All six of these vessels started their careers as sloops and were not fitted out as bombs until after 1741. This suggests that there were not as many operations in which bombs could participate as had been

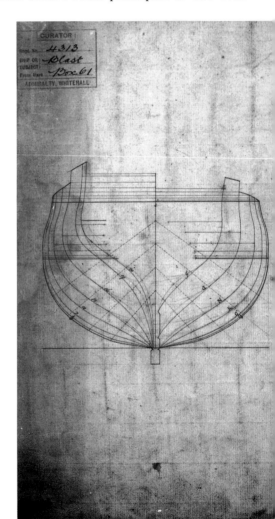

***Blast*, 1740, design lines and profile.**

Built to the line of the *Alderney*. The one feature which the *Blast* has which does not appear on the draught of the *Alderney* is a capstan on the quarterdeck. The capstan has obvious advantages over the windlass and given the need to use springs to warp the vessels into action it was a necessary refinement.

Table 18: *BLAST* CLASS, 1740, BUILT TO *ALDERNEY* LINES
Specification

Armament:	Mortars		Secondary	Men
Design	1 x 13in, 1 x 10in		6 x 4pdrs, 10 swivels	60
As completed	1 x 13in, 1 x 10in		6 x 4pdrs, 10 swivels	
As Sloops			10 x 4pdrs, 14 swivels	

	Gun deck ft-ins	Keel ft-ins	Breadth ft-ins	Depth in hold ft-ins	Burthen tons
Design					
As completed					
Blast	90-9	73-10½	26-3	10-11	270^{72}/$_{94}$
Basilisk	91-5	75-3½	26-0	10-11½	270^{69}/$_{94}$
Thunder	91-3	74-7	26-3	10-11¾	272^{28}/$_{94}$
Carcass	91-5	74-2	26-4¾	11-10	274^{43}/$_{94}$
Lighting	90-10	73-10·½	26-5½	11-0	275
Furnace	91-6	73-11^{7}/$_{8}$	26-4	11-0	272^{79}/$_{94}$

Building data

Name	Ordered	Builder	Laid down	Launched	Fate
Blast	11 Mar 1740	West	19 Mar 1740	28 Aug 1740	Taken 1745
Basilisk	11 Mar 1740	Snellgrove	3 Apr 1740	30 Aug 1740	Sold 1750
Thunder	11 Mar 1740	Bird	23 Apr 1740	30 Aug 1740	Foundered 1744
Carcass	11 Mar 1740	Taylor	23 Apr 1740	27 Sep 1740	Sold 1740
Lighting	11 Mar 1740	Bird	23 Apr 1740	24 Oct 1740	Foundered 1746
Furnace	11 Mar 1740	Quallett	23 Apr 1740	25 Oct 1740	Sold 1763

originally envisaged. Bombs did go with Vernon to the West Indies, but given that Britain's initial concentration was on Spanish overseas possessions, they would not be used against targets on the continent of Europe.

There are two sailing quality reports for bombs of this period, one for the *Salamander* of the 1730 group and one for the *Basilisk* of the 1740 group. The report for the *Salamander* is dated 23 October 1743, just a year before she was sold out of the service, but while it may not represent the ship in the peak of condition, the reports were retrospective and were intended to summarise the captain's whole experience of the ship. It is

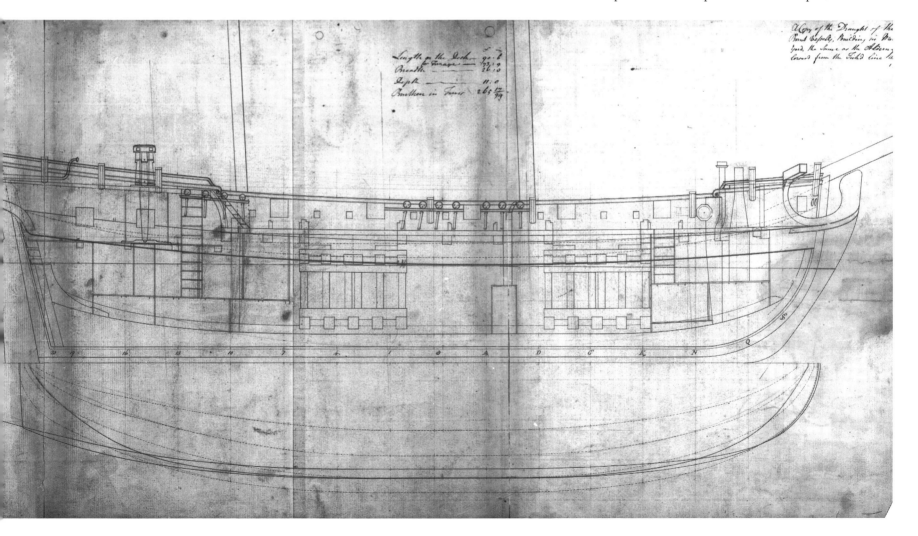

invaluable as it relates to a fairly early design and makes it possible to compare it with one of the standard designs of the mid century.

Table 19: SAILING QUALITIES OF THE *SALAMANDER*[53]

Her best sailing draught of water, when victualled and stored for Channel service 10ft 0in afore, 10ft 11in aft, or as much lighter (at the same difference) as she is able to bear sail. Her lowest gundeck ports will then be above the surface of the water —, after port —, fore ditto — .

Query the first. How she behaves close-hauled and how many knots she runs:

In a topgallant gale she carries her helm a turn to weather and runs 5kts

In a topsail gale she carries her helm a turn to weather and runs 5kts

How she steers, and how she wears and stays she steers well and wears and stays well

Under her reefed topsails one reef in, carries her helm a turn aweather and runs 4½ to 5kts; two reefs in, carries her helm a weather and runs 4½kts

reefed courses she carrys her helm amidships and runs 3½ and 4kts

And query, whether she will stay under her courses she stays indifferently

Query the 2nd. In each circumstance above mentioned (in sailing with other ships) in what proportion she gathers to windward, and in what proportion she forereaches, and in general her proportion of leeway she goes to windward with most ships or vessels in company; under double reefed topsails and a head sea two points leeway; under treble reefed topsails, a head sea two points and a half; under courses she makes three points leeway. In a topgallant or topsail gale half a point leeway

Query the 3rd. How she proves in sailing through all variations of the wind ... in every strength of gale... and how many knots she runs... and how she carries her helm two points abaft the beam and topsails, courses and staysails, in a fresh gale runs 7kts.

Wind on the beam, all sails set except stun sails, fresh wind and smooth water runs 6kts

Query the 4th. The most knots she runs before the wind, and how she rolls in the trough of the sea 8kts, rolls deep and heavy

Query the 5th. How she behaves lying too under a main sail and also under a mizzen balanced under a main sail falls off, rolls deep weather and sea heavy; under mizzen does not fall off so much, but rolls more quickly.

Query the 6th. What for a roader she is [How she rides at anchor] and how she careens She pitches very deep and rolls deep. Careens hard

....

Query the 10th. The trim of the ship Is my opinion near the above draught of water, from 9in to 11in by the stern, her mast being raked aft, which I have found has seen the best of her sailing either by the wind, large or before it

The *Basilisk* report is dated 24 May 1745.

Table 20: SAILING QUALITIES OF THE *BASILISK* [54]

Her best sailing draught of water, when victualled and stored for Channel service 12ft 6in afore, 13ft 6in aft, or as much lighter (at the same difference) as she is able to bear sail. Her lowest gundeck ports will then be above the surface of the water —, after port —, fore ditto — .

Query the first. How she behaves close-hauled and how many knots she runs:

In a topgallant gale 6½kts

In a topsail gale 5kts

How she steers, and how she wears and stays she steers very well during the time you can carry a main topsail

Under her reefed topsails 4½kts

reefed courses 2kts

And query, whether she will stay under her courses No

Query the 2nd. In each circumstance above mentioned (in sailing with other ships) in what proportion she gathers to windward, and in what proportion she forereaches, and in general her proportion of leeway Never in company with any other ships to try, and when could carry the main topsail never made above one point and a half leeway

Query the 3rd. How she proves in sailing through all variations of the wind ... in every strength of gale... and how many knots she runs ... and how she carries her helm [no entry]

Query the 4th. The most knots she runs before the wind, and how she rolls in the trough of the sea 11kts and rolls very easy in the sea

Query the 5th. How she behaves lying too under a main sail and also under a mizzen balanced never made a trial

Query the 6th. What for a roader she is [How she rides at anchor] and how she careens A very good roader, but very difficult to careen

....

Query the 10th. The trim of the ship Afore 11ft 6in, abaft 12ft 0in

It is unfortunate that the report is perfunctory and incomplete, but it does not preclude a comparison of the two designs which the *Salamander* and *Basilisk* represent. There was at this time no objective measure of wind and sea state, as was later developed into the Beaufort scale, so one ship's 'topgallant gale' (the strongest wind in which a ship could safely carry her topgallants) was not necessarily the same as another's. That having been said, the *Basilisk* was superior in terms of speed on all points of sailing, and in all sea states (except well reefed down). Compared with proper cruisers they were significantly slower, 8-9kts close-hauled and 11-12kts with the wind on the quarter being average for small frigates and sloops. *Basilisk* was less leewardly than *Salamander*, but again it is unlikely that either was as weatherly as a regular warship. *Basilisk* also rode to her anchors easier than the earlier ship, an important attribute in bomb vessels that fired from anchored positions. While speed was not an essential for a specialised vessel such as a bomb, such poor performance would have severely compromised their secondary role as sloops.

There is evidence of this shortcoming in a letter written by Captain Amherst who commanded the *Mortar*, one of the group built in 1741 to the *Alderney*'s lines: 'The many ill qualities of the sloop [she was fitted as a sloop during 1742-45] – she is low wasted and over masted.'[55] And Amherst goes on to say that under double reefed topsails and in any sea, 'she delves her forecastles under and carries her lee guns, wales underwater.'[56] The situation highlights the essential problem that specialist types often require features so extreme to carry out their main role that their subsidiary function can only come a poor second. As well as the issue of speed, *Salamander* was prone to roll excessively before

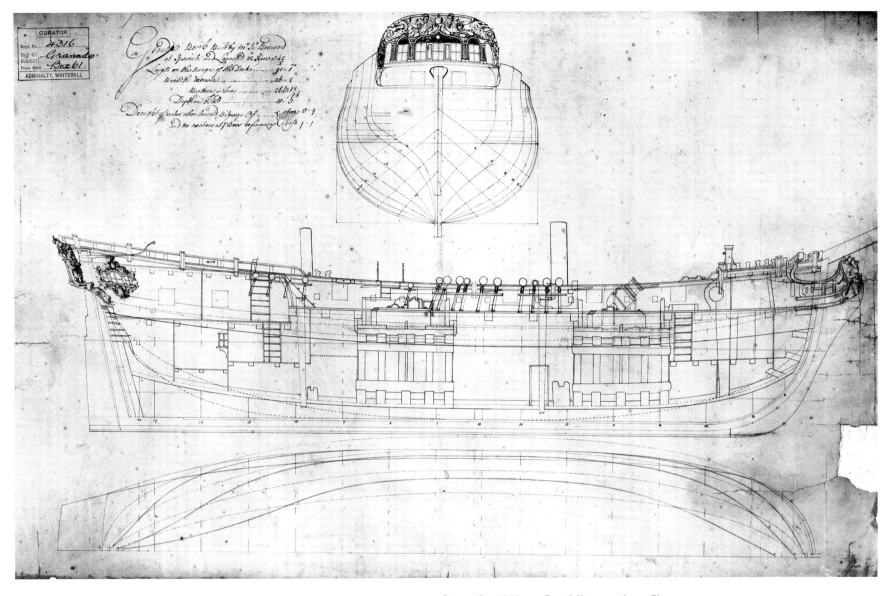

Granado, 1742, as fitted lines and profile.

The *Granado* was a development of the *Alderney* type but with full-width stern; the positioning of the main and mizzen masts was much the same, with the same resultant sailing characteristics. The position of the channels and deadeyes clearly illustrates the problems of the masking of the after mortar. The mortars are shown stowed (after) and in firing position (forward). The forward mortar has the wooden quoin used to raise it. Visible just aft of the break in the poop on the lower platform is the light for the magazine.

the wind – not unusual in square rigged ships – but *Basilisk* was easier on this point of sailing. The former was also very uncomfortable when riding at anchor, as she pitched as well. The fact of heavy pitching and rolling in any seaway is important given that the prime objective was to provide a stable firing platform for the mortars, so *Basilisk*'s easier motions must be regarded as a significant design improvement.[57]

Another example of their poor seakeeping qualities – although its significance should be treated with caution – is provided by what happened to the *Blast* in 1741. Captain Teacher 'represented that the *Blast* bomb vessel under his command pooped a sea at the Nore.'[58] Although the waters of the Nore anchorage can be rough, it is surprising to find an anchored vessel pooped in such circumstances. Taken with the evidence inferred from the sailing quality reports, it reinforces the view that these vessels were poor sea-boats.

There are also some insights to be gained into the building schedules

for the first series of vessels. There is Navy Board correspondence relating to the contracted deadlines for launching, and also to the debate over the type and numbers of mortars and cannon to be established for this group. The letter dated 2 April 1740 stated that the bombs were due for launching 'by the last spring tide in August'.[59]

By 2 July 1740 the Navy Board was writing to the Admiralty about the armament of these vessels.[60] This was to be one 10in and one 13in mortar and six 4pdr carriage guns. This does not agree with what is usually published for these vessels,[61] but this is definitely what was agreed between the Navy Board and the Admiralty. Subsequently Their Lordships reviewed this and the establishment was changed again. It is not possible to say whether the original armament was actually fitted.[62]

The captain of the *Thunder* (then acting as a sloop) wrote to the Navy Board in October of 1740 requesting that he might have two 6pdrs fitted in the great cabin of his vessel as chasers, and the same be fitted to the bombs building. If there was a problem the captain suggested that they could be placed 'to run out of the two ports in the bulkhead of the steerage.'[63]

It was at this period also that the benefits of the new types of mortars became clear. Up until about 1726 the mortars had been cast in one piece on their bases without trunnions, but the draughts of this group quite clearly show the new trunnion-mounted mortars, sometimes shown with one mortar housed parallel to the deck and one in the elevated firing position.

What is also clear from this correspondence is that by this date the Admiralty and the Navy Board were deciding how to equip these vessels rather than the Board of Ordnance, which had done so for many of the

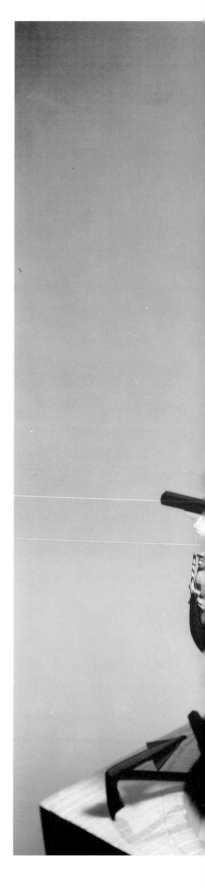

A modern model of the *Granado*, 1742.

The model was built in 1974 by R A Lightley of Cape Town and acquired by the National Maritime Museum after winning a ship model competition. The model is unplanked on the starboard side, and can be divided at the waterline to show the interior (see later). The model has one mortar uncovered and the other protected by the new hatch coverings introduced in the 1740s.

Table 21: *COMET* CLASS, 1741
Specification

Armament:	Mortars		Secondary		Men
Design	1 x 13in, 1 x 10in		8 x 4pdrs, 12 swivels		60
As completed	1 x 13in, 1 x 10in		8 x 4pdrs, 12 swivels		60
When rated as sloops			10 x 4pdrs and 14 swivels		

	Gun deck ft-ins	Keel ft-ins	Breadth ft-ins	Depth in hold ft-ins	Burthen tons
Design	91-0	75-6	26-0	11-3	270
As completed					
Comet	91-10	75-0⁷/₈	26-3¼	11-2	275⁵⁵/₉₄
Firedrake	91-5¾	76?	26-6⁷/₈	11-2¾	282⁸⁹/₉₄
Mortar	91-0	75-5¼	26-4¾	11-2	279⁵⁴/₉₄
Serpent	92-9	75-11³/₈	26-5	11-2½	274⁸¹/₉₄
Terror	91-9	74-11³/₈	26-1¼	11-2½	274⁸¹/₉₄

Building data

Name	Ordered	Builder	Laid down	Launched	Fate
Comet	14 Sep 1741	Taylor, Rotherhithe	8 Oct 1741	29 Mar 1742	Sold 1749
Firedrake	14 Sep 1741	Perry, Blackwall	7 Oct 1741	20 Feb 1742	Sold 1763
Mortar	14 Sep 1741	Perry, Blackwall	8 Oct 1741	25 Feb 1742	Sold 1749
Serpent	14 Sep 1741	Snellgrove, Limehouse	9 Oct 1741	15 Mar 1742	Wrecked 1748
Terror	14 Sep 1741	Greville	9 Oct 1741	13 Mar 1742	Sold 1754

first bombs, as outlined earlier. This is a signal change as it suggests far closer integration between the weapon and its carrier – the mortars and the bomb vessel – than would have been possible with earlier designs.

The next group were once again built to the lines of the *Alderney*, although with further very slight modifications to the dimensions (see Table 21). This implies a basic satisfaction with the design rather than bureaucratic inertia, since contemporary sloops were subject to almost constant modification.

A month after this batch had been ordered, in November 1741, the Admiralty wrote to the Navy Board to ask once again what was to be the armament of these vessels and also the arrangement and dimensions of the ports (information which had to be passed to the Board of Ordnance in order to construct the carriages accurately): 'The height of the port cills are in the waists one foot and six inches and in the fall abaft [the drop of the deck level aft to give the cabin reasonable headroom] one foot ten inches.'[64]

The proposed armament when fitted as a sloop shows that the request of the *Thunder*'s captain had been adopted by the Navy Board and these ships were allowed stern chasers of 6pdr calibre.[65]

Carriage guns	4pdrs – 5ft 6in – in the waists	10
Carriage guns	6pdrs – 6ft long – for the fall abaft	2
Swivels	½pdr – 3ft long	14

As finally settled the armament was:

| As a bomb | eight 5ft 6in 4pdrs, plus fourteen ½pdr swivels |
| As a sloop | ten 5ft 6in 4pdrs, plus fourteen ½pdr swivels plus two 6ft 0in 6pdrs |

The five vessels which were launched in 1742 were almost immediately converted for their secondary role as sloops. In June of that year the Navy Board sent the Admiralty an estimate of the time, cost and nature of the proposed conversion. It is worth quoting the letter at length as it shows the compromises which had to be made in the design to gain the dual function.

> *Terror* and six employed as sloops without removing the bomb beds. But it will be necessary to take down the side of the shell room and the carlings and pillars next the side to make room in the hold for lodging of the men and stowing provisions.[66]

Also outlined was the need to cover the mortar beds with hatches. The cost for this work was estimated at £100 and it would take fifteen days to complete in the yard at Deptford.[67]

To restore the vessel to her role as a bomb it was further estimated that it would take twelve days and cost some £160. Whether the hatches constructed fitted flush to the deck or were similar to those on the *Granado* is not specified. What is certain is that the yard officers were alive to the problem of the mortar beds and how to keep them dry, at least when the vessels were in use as sloops. Another consequence of the work undertaken at this time was that all six vessels were given a new complement of men when acting as sloops, 100 when operating in the Channel and 110 when on foreign service.

There are no sailing quality reports for this group, but with very similar hull form and rig they must have had the same the broad characteristics as reported for the *Basilisk*.

Just before a new phase of the war came about in 1744, with the entrance of France into the conflict, more bombs were fitted out for service, during which one of the prewar bombs was surveyed. The result was that the *Salamander* was taken into dockyard hands and it was found that it would take £2350 to repair her and make her fit for service.[68] This was two-thirds of the construction cost of the *Infernal* class built in the 1750s, the average cost of which was £3700 for the hulls, masts and rigging. The result of this inspection was the Admiralty decision that the *Salamander* should be sold out of the service. Just as the older vessels were showing signs of hard service, so the group built in 1740 were exhibiting some problems. The captain of the *Lightning* complained to the Navy Board that she was leaky, attributing the prime reason for this to the weight of her mortars and the 'tauntness' [height] of her masts.[69]

Not all problems could be placed at the door of the design or builders. In 1744, not long after fitting out as a bomb, the *Terror* ran aground at Birling Gap a little before midday on 2 April 1744. It took five days to float her off and she had to be docked in May to repair the damage, which consisted of having all her sheathing rubbed off. This necessitated her remaining out of commission until June of 1744.[70]

The last vessel purpose built as a bomb during this war was the *Granado*,[71] ordered in 1741 and launched in 1742. She differed from her near sisters in that she had a full square stern which replaced the narrow pink stern which had been the norm for all bombs since 1695. She also had the refinement of the first recorded permanent hatches over her mortar beds. In terms of rig she differed little from the ketch sail plan of her near sisters built to the *Alderney*'s lines.

There is a sailing report, albeit undated, which gives some indication of whether the modified stern, with its slightly fuller hull form, had any effect on sailing qualities.

Table 22: *GRANADO* CLASS, 1741
Specification

Armament:	Mortars		Secondary		Men
Design	1 x 13in, 1 x 10in		8 x 4pdrs plus 12 swivels		60
As completed	1 x 13in, 1 x 10in		8 x 4pdrs plus 12 swivels		60

	Gun deck ft-ins	Keel ft-ins	Breadth ft-ins	Depth in hold ft-ins	Burthen tons
Design	91-1	73-10¼	26-2	11-4	268⁹²/₉₄
As completed					
Granado	91-1	74-1½	26-2	11-3	270

Building data

Name	Ordered	Builder	Laid Down	Launched	Fate
Granado	14 Sep 1741	Barnard, Ipswich	18 Nov 1741	22 Jun 1742	Sold 1763

Table 23: SAILING QUALITIES OF *GRANADO*[72]

Her best sailing draught of water, when victualled and stored for Channel service 12ft 5in **afore,** 11ft 6in **aft, or as much lighter (at the same difference) as she is able to bear sail. Her lowest gundeck ports will then be above the surface of the water —, after port —, fore ditto — .**

Query the first. How she behaves close-hauled and how many knots she runs:

In a topgallant gale very well and runs 7½kts

In a topsail gale very well and runs 7½kts

How she steers, and how she wears and stays she both steers, wears and stays well

Under her reefed topsails behaves well and runs 4½kts

reefed courses [no entry]

And query, whether she will stay under her courses will not

Query the 2nd. In each circumstance above mentioned (in sailing with other ships) in what proportion she gathers to windward, and in what proportion she forereaches, and in general her proportion of leeway does not gather so much to windward or forereach so much in a topgallant gale as she does under lower sails and hold as good a wind as most other ships

Query the 3rd. How she proves in sailing through all variations of the wind ... in every strength of gale... and how many knots she runs.. and how she carries her helm proves a tolerable good sailer through all variations of the wind from being a point or two abaft the beam, veering forward on a bowline in every strength of gale but best in a stiff gale and behaves well in a head sea. With the wind on or a little abaft the beam runs 9kts but not so much in a head sea; carries her helm pretty well.

Query the 4th. The most knots she runs before the wind, and how she rolls in the trough of the sea runs 10kts before the wind and rolls easy

Query the 5th. How she behaves lying too under a main sail and also under a mizzen balanced lies to under a main or balanced mizzen very well

Query the 6th. What for a roader she is [How she rides at anchor] and how she careens very good roader, careens tolerable well

....

Query the 10th. The trim of the ship her rigging not too taut and her masts upright

In comparison with the group built directly from the lines of the *Alderney*, the *Granado* seems to have been a rather easier sea-boat on the evidence of this one report. She appears to be not quite as fast as the *Basilisk*, which registered 11kts before the wind, but within the crude measurements of the time the difference is probably insignificant. It is an assertion that needs to be heavily qualified, but there does seem to be a gradual improvement in the qualities of the vessels. Unlike the 1741 group, there is no suggestion of the ship being over-masted. Her sailing qualities take on greater significant when it is realised that for fourteen years out of the twenty-one *Granado* was in service she was rigged as a sloop. This was in part due to the fact that most of her commissions were in peacetime, but it again highlights the question of whether it was cost effective to build on purpose rather than to adapt other vessels for bomb duties as and when required.

The construction of the *Granado* threw up some problems typical of wartime construction programmes. The ship was delivered late and the Navy Board sought to deduct part of the payment as a penalty. Her builder, Barnard of Ipswich, naturally objected, pointing out by way of explanation that his shipwrights had been tempted away to be ship's carpenters in the *Hampshire* (a 50-gun ship also built by Barnard, then fitting out at Ipswich). Since the Navy itself was partly to blame, Their Lordships took pity on Mr Barnard and allowed the whole price to be paid.[73]

In general the bombs built during this period can be seen as a maturing of the elements which had been there from the beginning. Apart from the trunnioned mortar, there were no new and startling developments which radically separated the bomb from its prototypes of sixty years earlier, and even size did not grow dramatically. This gradual improvement had its drawbacks in as much as seakeeping seemed to remain a problem, while the dual function of the vessels built to the finer lines of the *Alderney* emphasised the competing elements of cruiser versus mortar platform. Nor was the rig of the vessel changed substantially during this period, which limited possible improvements in both speed and seakeeping. It would have to wait for the next war for many of these issues to be addressed.

As well as the vessels which survived the rigours of war and weather to see service in the next conflict, there were several sloops built in the period leading up to the war of 1739 which were converted in the 1750s to bombs, but for the sake of chronology these will be dealt with in the next chapter.

Table 24 : FATES OF SURVIVING BOMB VESSELS

Name	Fate
Salamander	Sold 1744
Terrible	Sold 1749
Alderney	Hulked 1742
1740 GROUP	
Basilisk	Sold 1750
Blast	Taken near Jamaica 19 Oct 1745
Carcass	Sold 1749
Furnace	Sold 1763
Lighting	Capsized off Leghorn 16 Jun 1746
Thunder	Wrecked at Jamaica in a hurricane 20 Oct 1744
1741 GROUP	
Comet	Sold 1749
Firedrake	Sold 1763
Mortar	Sold 1749
Serpent	Wrecked near Barbados 1 Sep 1748
Terror	Sold 1754
Granado	Sold 1763

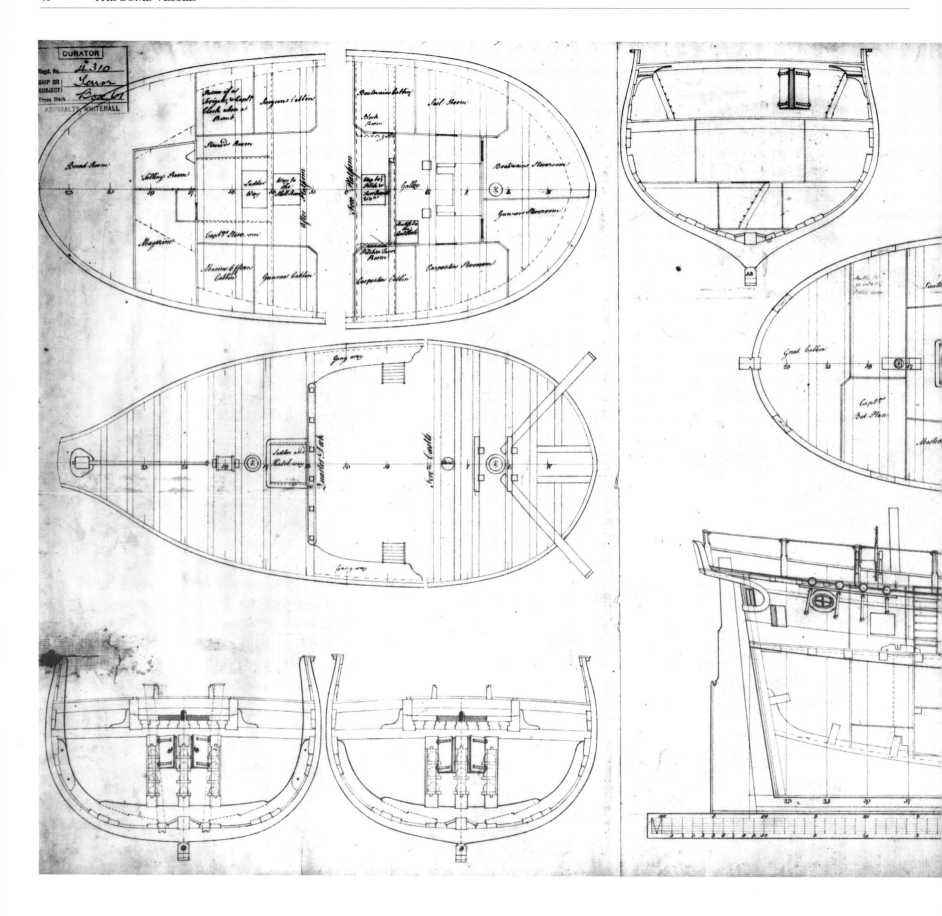

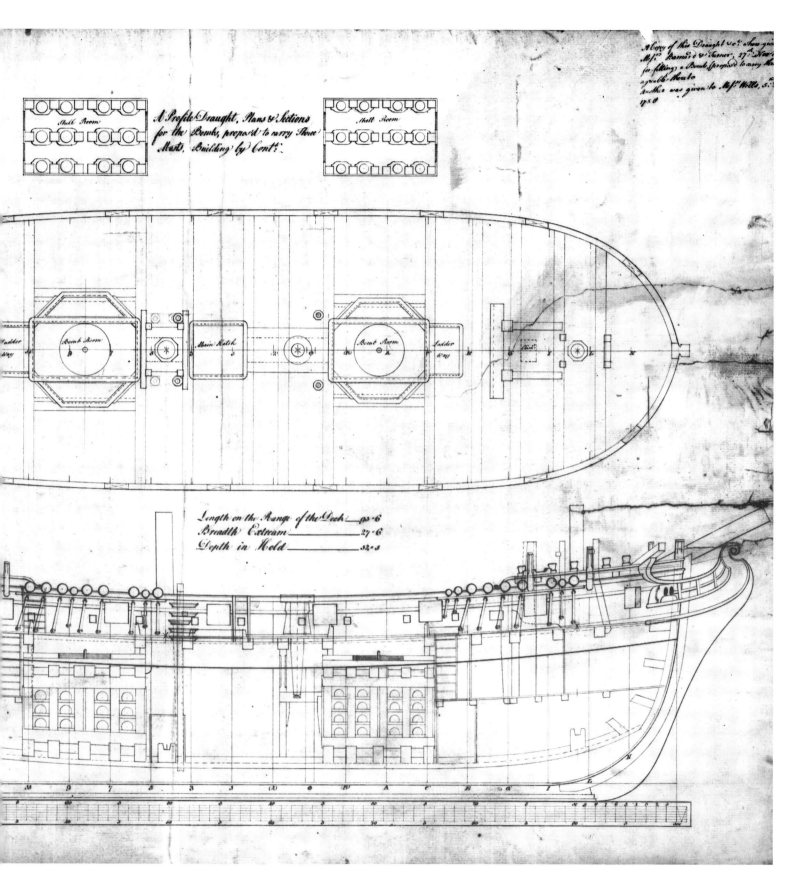

A Profile Draught, Plans & Sections for the Bombs, prepar'd to carry Three Masts, Building by Cont.

Shell Room

Bomb Room

Main Hatch

Bomb Room

Ladder

Length on the Range of the Deck _____ 93·6
Breadth Extream _____ 27·6
Depth in Hold _____ 12·5

Infernal class (ship rigged), 1757, lines, profile, decks and sections.

The weight of the mortars and shell rooms was more evenly spread in this class than had been the case in earlier vessels. There was still the problem with the aft mortar being masked by the standing rigging for the main mast. This draught was for the vessels of this class which were to be ship rigged, the first bombs since 1693 to carry three masts. The mizzen is just forward of the wheel on the quarterdeck. The section through the mortar beds demonstrates the structure of these vessels, something which militated against their being fast sailors. The vessels built during the American Revolutionary War were built to the same lines, so like the *Alderney*s they can be seen to be satisfactory designs.

5. *The Seven Years War*

THE PERIOD OF PEACE WAS barely a decade between settling the War of Austrian Succession and the outbreak of what became known as the Seven Years War in 1757. In this short time, however, many of the bombs built for the previous conflict had disappeared from the service. Their fates were given in Table 24.

From the above list it is apparent that all but three of the previously built bomb vessels had gone by the outbreak of war. This allowed the designer almost a clean slate to bring in major changes and build on the experience gained with the previous classes without producing a fleet of mixed capabilities. In strategic terms Britain was to follow a policy of attacking French colonies while subsidising allied armies to fight on the Continent. Assistance to the latter was provided by diversionary amphibious descents on the coast, as had taken place in William's war in the 1690s, and an integral part of this, as with the earlier campaign, was to be the widespread use of the bomb vessel. Hence both technically and strategically the time was right for the next phase in the development of the British bomb vessel.

The main new feature of the class of bombs built in this war was the

Blast, 1757, design profile for ketch rigged vessels.

The *Blast*, *Mortar* and *Thunder* were ketch rigged versions of the *Infernal* design. The mizzen is on the break of the quarterdeck and the capstan is sited just forward of the quarterdeck (it is amidships on the ship rigged vessels). The positioning of the bomb beds is different in the ketch and ship rigged half-sisters to accommodate the stepping of the masts.

Table 25: *INFERNAL* CLASS, 1756
Specification

Armament:	Mortars	Secondary	Men
Design	1 x 13in, 1 x 10in	8 x 6pdr, 14 swivels	60
As completed	1 x 13in, 1 x 10in	8 x 6pdr, 14 swivels	
When fitted as sloops		14 x 6pdr, 14 swivels	110

	Gun deck ft-ins	Keel ft-ins	Breadth ft-ins	Depth in hold ft-ins	Burthen tons
Design	91-6	74-1¼	27-6	12-1	298^{22}/$_{94}$
As completed					
Infernal	91-9	75-0^{5}/$_{8}$	27-9	12-1	307
Blast	91-6	74-0	27-9	12-1	303^{10}/$_{94}$
Thunder	91-6	74-2	27-8	12-1	302
Mortar	92-0	74-8	28-1	12-1	313
Carcass	91-8	74-2^{3}/$_{8}$	28-0	12-1½	309^{39}/$_{94}$
Basilisk	91-7	74-4	28-1	12-1½	311^{90}/$_{94}$
Terror	91-6	74-2	27-8	12-1	302

Building data

Name	Ordered	Builder	Laid down	Launched	Fate
Infernal	5 Oct 1756	West	Nov 1756	4 Jul 1757	Sold 1774
Blast	21 Sep 1758	H Bird	Oct 1758	27 Feb 59	BU 1771
Thunder	21 Sep 1758	Hennikar	16 Oct 1758	12 Mar 59	Sold 1774
Mortar	21 Sep 1758	Wells	2 Oct 1758	14 Mar 1759	Sold 1774
Carcass	21 Sep 1758	Stanton	28 Sep 1758	27 Jan 1759	Sold 1784
Basilisk	21 Sep 1758	Wells	2 Oct 1758	10 Feb 1759	Taken 1762
Terror	21 Sep 1758	Bale	13 Oct 1758	16 Jan 1759	Sold 1774

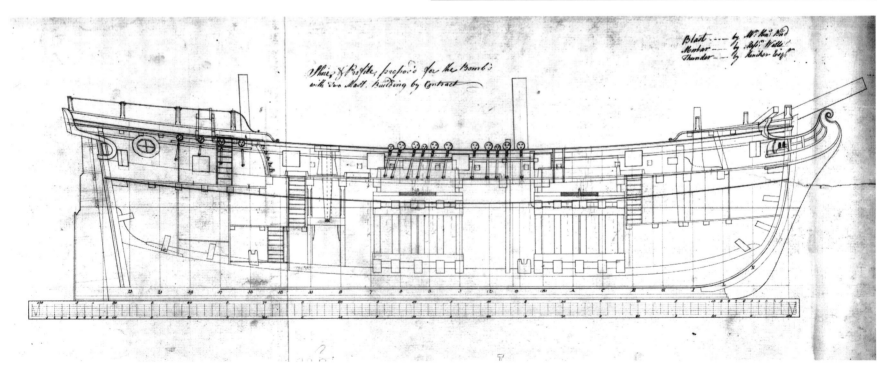

three-masted ship rig, the first departure from the ketch, which had been standard for all previous vessels barring the *Mortar* class of the 1690s. The sailing reports referred to earlier show that, although some individual vessels had good points of sailing, on balance even the *Alderney*s were not the handiest vessels, and the ketch rig had much to with this. It also limited them in their subsidiary functions, and it is significant that sloops – which hitherto had been either snow or ketch rigged – were also being experimentally rigged as ships at about this time. For bombs the balance of the rig, even when operating as a sloop, was a compromise due to the position of the masts being determined by the mortar beds. However, all two-masted vessels were inherently more vulnerable in action than three-masted ships, since the loss of fewer spars would cripple them. Furthermore,

brigs, snows and ketches were also less handy, because the fore- and aftersail on a ship could provide more leverage in manouevring. These points were made by the Navy Board in its proposal to the Admiralty:

> It having been observed that the bombs and other vessels of their burden rigged as ketches are not so manageable in bad weather, nor do they work so readily and certain in narrow places as vessels of the

Blast, 1757, design deck plans and sections for ketch rigged vessels.

With the exception of the rig the internal layout of the *Blast* and her sisters was the same as the ship rigged *Infernal*s, except that the bomb rooms were closer together in the ketches.

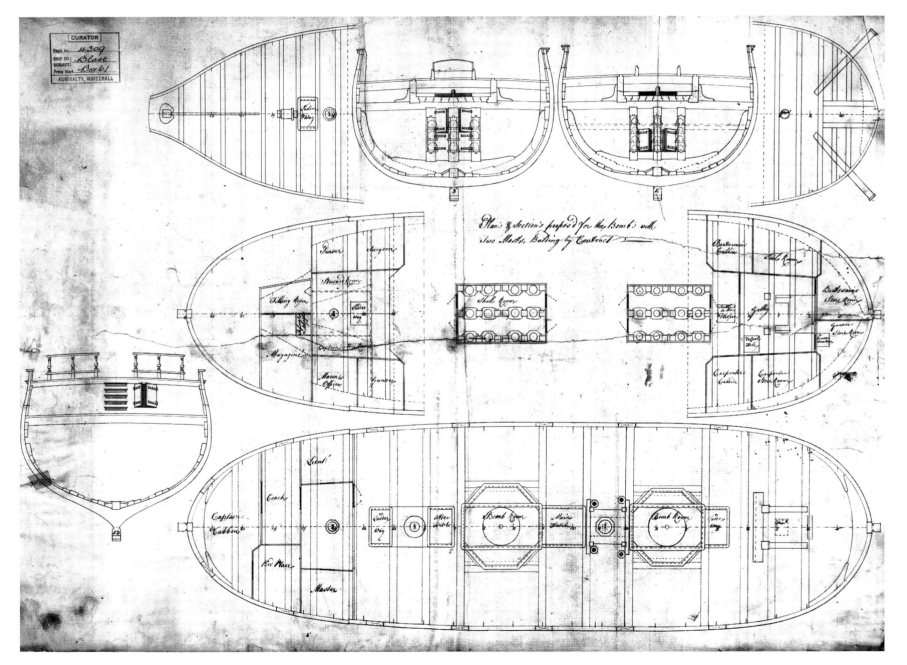

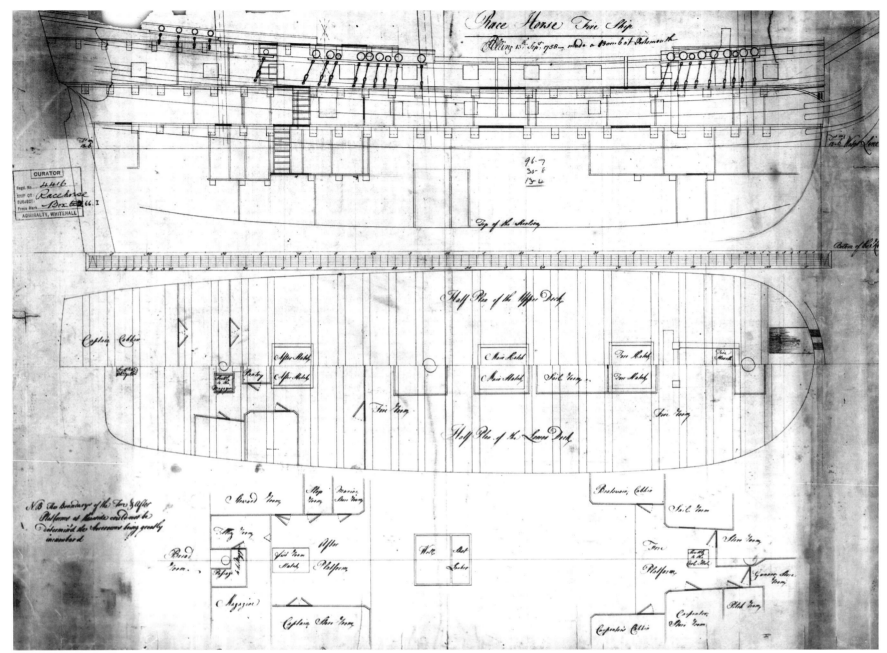

***Racehorse*, 1757, profile and deck plan for fitting as a fireship.**

This captured vessel had a long and varied career in the Royal Navy. She was first fitted as a fireship, but this draught notes '18 Sept 1758 – made a bomb at Portsmouth'.

same size rigged with three masts – and as three of the six bombs now building by contract have their mortars and works so disposed that they may receive three masts or two as ketches, and have in all other respects so far as we can discover at present the free use of the said mortars in either state and to appearance will be less incumbered with rigging with three masts than as ketches and which being also more suitable to their service as frigates, if at any time they be

appointed to act as such, we herewith send you two draughts, one representing a bomb with her lower masts and mortars disposed as usual to sail as a ketch, the other representing with three masts, and desire you will lay the same before the Right Honble the Lords Commrs of the Admiralty and that you will propose to their Lordships that a trial may be made of three of the said bombs rigged with three masts and the other three as ketches...

There was no argument about the merits of the proposal and the Admiralty order for the first group, dated 8 November 1758, specifies that three are to be ketches and three ship rigged 'by way of trial'.[74] There are some sailing quality reports for these vessel which will be discussed later in the chapter.

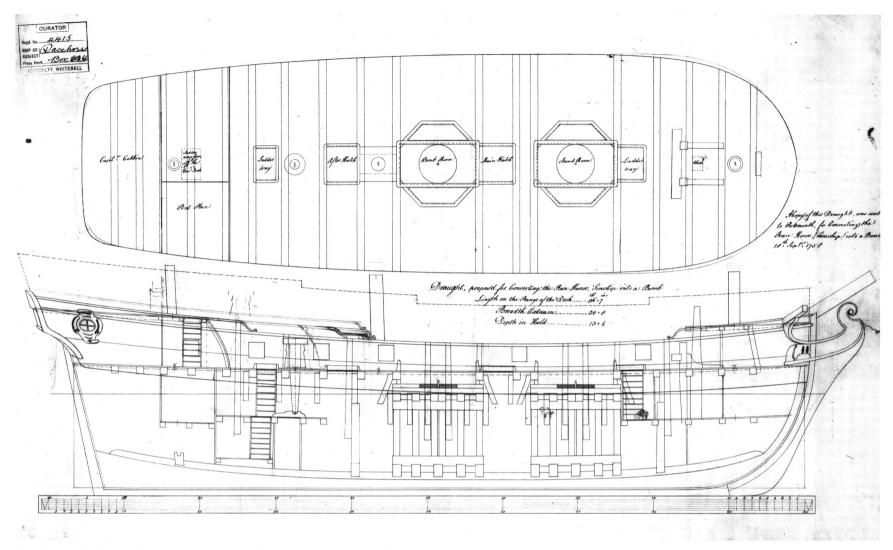

Racehorse, 1757, profile and deck plan for fitting as a bomb, dated 18 September 1758.

This draught shows just how much work was involved in *Racehorse*'s conversion into a bomb vessel. The principal difference is that the topside has been cut down by a deck and the main mast moved aft to step abaft both mortars which would have been an advantage. She also has the double wheel set just aft of the mizzen on the quarterdeck as well as a capstan just forward of it.

Table 25 lists the vessels of what was to be called the *Infernal* class after the lead vessel, and also includes the repeat vessels built in 1770s to the same design. All bombs built after this date were to be ships – *ie* three-masted – so it can be safely assumed that the comparative trial proved the superiority of the ship rig over the ketch. With reference to the sail plan it is interesting that when not rigged as bombs this class were described as 'frigates'.[75] This term was also applied to the new three-masted sloops, so may mean little more than 'ship rigged' in this context, but it does suggest a stronger identification with a cruising role.

In term of dimensions the length on the deck was not changed from the *Granado* and her half-sisters nor the length on the keel, but the beam was increased by some 16ins over both the *Granado* and the *Alderney*s, producing an increase in the burthen of some 30 tons over their predecessors. Together with a rather fuller hull form, this strongly indicates that stability was a problem with the earlier classes.

For the *Infernal*s it is possible to give a complete breakdown of how much each vessel cost to build (barring only the *Blast*, which was sold in 1771) and how much was spent on them during their careers. These costs of building are set out below:

Table 26: BUILDING COSTS FOR THE *INFERNAL* CLASS[76]

Name	Cost of hull and rigging
Infernal	£3355
Carcass	£3758
Mortar	£3758
Terror	£3579
Thunder	£3579

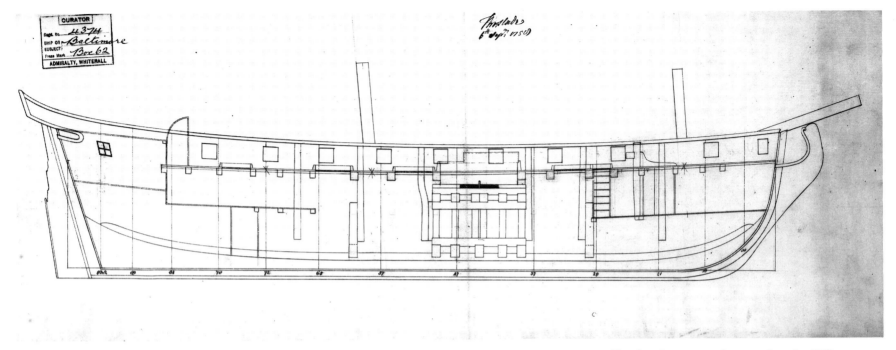

Baltimore, 1742, profile plan for conversion to a bomb, 1758.

When the *Baltimore* was converted to a bomb in 1758 she carried only one mortar; this may have been due in part to problems with her stability, as is explained in the text, since she had a fine-lined sloop hull form.

Construction in merchant yards was contracted on a £ per ton basis, with the final instalment of payment being dependent on a careful measurement of the hull as completed. This is why there is always some slight variation in the listed dimensions of vessels built in merchant yards to the same draught, but equally why the construction prices are often very similar when based on the same price per ton. It is interesting to see how much the price of these vessel had increased over the first bomb vessels. Using the slightly higher price quoted, the total cost for the first seven of the *Infernal*s would have been £25,048. This is for the hull and fittings only; the costs for the ordnance have not been found for these vessels but it can be assumed that they would be in the same order of magnitude as for early bombs.

In that context in Chapter 1 the estimate for the *Firedrake* was given as £2828 for one vessel. The cost for the same number as the *Infernal*s would have been £19,796, a difference of 27 per cent for vessels which were only 7 per cent larger. While there was little long-term inflation during the eighteenth century, wartime shortages produced localised price rises, so the difference in the two sets of prices could perhaps be put down to the fact that the *Infernal*s were built by competitive tender on the open market, whereas the *Firedrake*s were to be built in the royal dockyards. Besides the capital costs of construction, bombs needed to be maintained, and since they usually required refitting after every action, they were a costly commitment. Based on the Progress Books, a complete breakdown of the costs of repairs and refits throughout the careers of the *Infernal* class is given in Table 27.

From this it can be seen that it cost on average another £400 to fit them for service. It is likely that this was for the fitting of the mortar beds themselves, which appears to have been a separate operation from the building of the hulls and rigging the vessels for sea. This cost has to be added to the total cost of hulls and fittings and makes just under £4000 for the cost of the new *Infernal*s before they were equipped with their ordnance and had fired a shot in anger.

With the exception of the *Carcass* what is also noticeable is the lack of investment in these vessels after the war ceased. The expenditure of between £20 and £30 in all probability reflects the minor cost of keeping them in the Ordinary (reserve). The only vessel for which there is a cost of refitting for service after a long sojourn in Ordinary is the *Carcass*. She was to be used for exploration and therefore the cost probably includes some special conversion work, but at some £1500, this was about 30 per cent of the original cost of building the vessel in the first

Table 27: MAINTENANCE COSTS OF THE *INFERNAL* CLASS[77]

Infernal	fitted 1757 £310 Po, 1758 Po £294, Po 1760 £493, Po 1761 repair £72, Po 1763 £20, Po 1772 £22.
Carcass	fitted 1759 £422 D, Po 1759 £273, Sh 1762 £139, D 1764 small repair £720, D 1765 £1249, D 1772 £190, Sh fitted and doubled £1192, D 1775 fitted £346, W 1775 as a bomb £1505, Po 1776 £227
Mortar	fitted 1759 £405, Po 1759 £296, Po 1760 £80, Po 1760 £121, Po 1761 £82, Ply 1761 refitted £170, Ply 1762 refitted £243, D 1764 £29, 1765 expense £16
Terror	W 1759 refitted £103, D 1764 small repair £1226, D 1765 expense £38, D 1770
Thunder	Ch 1759 fitted £542, Po 1760 refitted £98, Ply 1761 £27, Po 1761 fitted £214, D 1763 expense £18

Abbreviations: Ch-Chatham, D-Deptford, Po-Portsmouth, Ply-Plymouth, Sh-Sheerness.

place. This makes an interesting contrast with the case of the *Salamander*, which was sold to be broken up when it was estimated that it would cost over £3000 to repair her.

For two of the vessels which were built to the same lines in 1778 there are some comparative costs. The vessels in question, *Terror* and *Thunder*, cost respectively £4882 and £4822 for their hulls and stores, which was an increase of roughly £1300 over their predecessors. Seen in these terms it would have made some sense to repair and put into service any of the 1750s vessels which were still in a state to be refitted. However, for small craft the Navy Board and Admiralty worked on the assumption that it was almost as fast to build a new hull as to repair one which had been in Ordinary for some time, particularly as repairs were almost exclusively the preserve of the royal dockyards, which had other priorities in wartime. Judging by the money spent on the *Infernal*s after the war was over, bombs and other minor craft were sacrificed to the exigences of peacetime budgetting.

As well as purpose-built bomb vessels, during the Seven Years War resort was made once again to conversion from vessels already in service or captured from the enemy. Table 28 lists both conversions of Royal Navy vessels and those bought in or captured and then converted.

The *Baltimore* and the *Pelican* reverted, in terms of armament, to the seventeenth century in that they mounted just one 13in mortar apiece. The *Racehorse* was to have a long and distinguished career both as a bomb and exploration vessel. She carried the now standard fit of one 13in and one 10in mortar, as did the *Falcon* and *Kingfisher*. There is some evidence that the over-masting which troubled the *Alderney* and her half-sisters was experienced by the *Pelican*. It was explained by the captain in a letter to the Navy Board which also gives a clue as to the type of conversion she underwent at Sheerness.

In essence the *Pelican* when she was fitted as a bomb stepped the same masts as when she had two decks, implying that the conversion involved cutting the ship down by a deck. As a result the lower masts were complained of as being too tall, so the ship could not get her tacks onboard; there was also the problem that the foot of the topsails touched the stays. There appears to have been some attempt to shorten the masts by the same amount as the vessel was altered: 'What was taken off from the height of the ship was nearly the same as what the mast was shortened, the courses were continued the same as before.'[78] This would make more sense if the problem had arisen during the ship's conversion to a sloop, but the date is clearly in the middle of her service as a bomb. In all event the problems of making a mortar-bearing hull into a reasonable sailing vessel was not just confined to the purpose-built vessels.

The converted ships had a variety of rigs, including snow for the *Baltimore* and *Kingfisher* (a novelty for bomb vessels), the more conventional ketch for *Falcon*, and ship for the bought in vessels. Although there is no surviving sailing report for the *Pelican*, there is a sailing report for the *Baltimore*, which whilst not a merchant conversion was one of the single-mortar vessels. She was also comparatively elderly when she was converted, being sixteen years old. Thus she make a good contrast with the *Infernal*s, for which there are some surviving reports.

Table 28: VESSELS CONVERTED TO BOMBS 1755-63
Specification

Armament:	Mortars		Secondary		Men
Design					
As completed					
Baltimore	1 x 13in		12 swivels		
Falcon	1 x 13in, 1 x 10in				
Kingfisher	1 x 13in, 1 x 10in				
Pelican	1 x 13in		8 x 4pdr, 12 swivels		60
Racehorse	1 x 13in, 1 x 10in		8 x 6pdr, 12 swivels		

	Gun deck ft-ins	Keel ft-ins	Breadth ft-ins	Depth in hold ft-ins	Burthen tons
Design					
As completed					
Baltimore	89-0	73-10	25-3¼	10-6	251
Falcon	91-?		26		270
Kingfisher	92		26		275
Pelican	86-10½	71-7½	24-5	11-1	234
Racehorse	96-7	77-1¼	30-8	13-4	385

Building data

Name	Builder	Launched	Fitted as Bomb	Fate
Baltimore	West, Deptford	30 Dec 1742	1758	Sold 1762
Falcon	Alexander, Thames	30 Nov 1745	1758	Wrecked 1759
Kingfisher	Darly, Gosport	12 Dec 1745	1758	Served as bomb 1758-60, sold 1763
*Pelican**		1758		Sold May 1763
Racehorse†		1757		Taken 1778

Notes: *Pelican* was merchant *Saint George*; she served as a sloop 1760-62. †*Racehorse*, captured privateer *Le Marquis de Vaudreuil*, exploration vessel 1773, 1775 bomb (renamed *Thunder*).

Table 29: SAILING QUALITIES OF THE *BALTIMORE*[79]
December 1762

Her best sailing draught of water, when victualled and stored for Channel service 11ft 0in afore, 10ft 4in aft, or as much lighter (at the same difference) as she is able to bear sail. Her lowest gundeck ports will then be above the surface of the water —, after port —, fore ditto — .

Query the first. How she behaves close-hauled and how many knots she runs:

In a topgallant gale she goes 7kts

In a topsail gale she goes 9kts

How she steers, and how she wears and stays steers easy and works very well

Under her reefed topsails 5kts

reefed courses 4kts **And query, whether she will stay under her courses** no trial

Query the 2nd. In each circumstance above mentioned (in sailing with other ships) in what proportion she gathers to windward, and in what proportion she forereaches, and in general her proportion of leeway if not over pressed by sail she will both weather and forereach

Query the 3rd. How she proves in sailing through all variations of the wind ... in every strength of gale... and how many knots she runs.. and how she carries her helm she behaves well in all variations of the wind. Carries a stiff sail and her helm generally half a turn a weather, and pitches easy in a head sea

Query the 4th. The most knots she runs before the wind, and how she rolls in the trough of the sea goes 9½, but very easy to her rigging

Query the 5th. How she behaves lying too under a main sail and also under a mizzen balanced lies to very badly in a great sea, under a fore and main sailor fore sail

Query the 6th. What for a roader she is [How she rides at anchor] and how she careens a great roader, but never careened

....

Query the 10th. The trim of the ship in my opinion 8ins by the head, the main mast with a great rake aft and the fore mast upright; goes best out of harbour with her hold full

In terms of general performance the *Baltimore* seems to have sailed well, which is to be expected of a sloop hull, and did not exhibit the tendency of the purpose-built vessel to pitch and roll heavily in any kind of seaway, perhaps because one mortar was a more reasonable burden for a vessel with a relatively sharp hull form. She also had a fair turn of speed, especially on a wind: 9kts close-hauled in a topsail gale is creditable, although she was somewhat slower than the best performer of the previous class before the wind, which could make 11kts. The fact that she could not be pressed and prefered to be stored deep suggests that her stability was sensitive, which probably explains why *Baltimore* only mounted the one mortar instead of the two which would have been usual for a vessel of her size.

By way of comparison there are some sailing reports for the *Infernal* class, both of the first group, and for those built in the 1770s. Of these, there is one for a ketch rigged vessel, so some idea can be gleaned of its performance relative to the ship's ketch rigged half-sisters. However, since no more ketch rigged bombs were built, it is a reasonable assumption that the ship rig was regarded as a significant improvement.

The ketch was the *Thunder* built in 1759 and the report is dated 1763, towards the end of her active service.

Table 30: SAILING QUALITIES OF THE *THUNDER*
24 June 1763

Her best sailing draught of water, when victualled and stored for Channel service — afore, — aft, or as much lighter (at the same difference) as she is able to bear sail. Her lowest gundeck ports will then be above the surface of the water 6ft 0in, after port 6ft 2in, fore ditto 6ft 4in.

Query the first. How she behaves close-hauled and how many knots she runs:

In a topgallant gale very stiff and will go 6kts

In a topsail gale very stiff and will go 6kts

How she steers, and how she wears and stays

she steers very easy, rather carries a lee helm for which reason we seldom make use of the standing jib on the wind. She wears very well and also stays quick in smooth water, but cannot depend on her staying in a rough sea

Under her reefed topsails not experienced

reefed courses not experienced

And query, whether she will stay under her courses [no entry]

Query the 2nd. In each circumstance above mentioned (in sailing with other ships) in what proportion she gathers to windward, and in what proportion she forereaches, and in general her proportion of leeway we were never weathered by any ships except His Majesties ships *Dublin* and *Dragon* and *Limerick*; we weathered the generality at the rate of a mile in four hours, but [did] not forereach anything to be mentioned, and we generally allow her in the first case 1 point, in the second 1½ and the third 2½ points leeway

Query the 3rd. How she proves in sailing through all variations of the wind ... in every strength of gale... and how many knots she runs ... and how she carries her helm she proves very lively before the wind, she will go with the wind one point abaft the beam 9½kts, the wind on the beam the same, and one point before the beam 8kts; she carries her helm one turn aweather

Query the 4th. The most knots she runs before the wind, and how she rolls in the trough of the sea she will go at particular times 10½kts; she rolls very deep

Query the 5th. How she behaves lying too under a main sail and also under a mizzen balanced not experienced

Query the 6th. What for a roader she is [How she rides at anchor] and how she careens never had occasion to try an anchor of her at an anchor in a great sea. She careens very stiff and without a spar deck she must get the forefoot out of the water

....

Query the 10th. The trim of the ship Best draught afore 12ft 4in, abaft 12ft 3in; taut rigging, the main mast 2½ins from the crosstrees of the gallows when it is arched as it is now

A significant change with this class was the method of steering. By the time the *Infernal*s were built the tiller had been replaced with a wheel. The draught for the *Basilisk* and *Carcass* quite clearly shows a wheel on the quarterdeck. This plus the change in rig potentially allowed better control of the vessels.

On the whole the *Thunder* could outperform her predecessors in terms of speed, being a knot or two faster on most points of sailing. It is claimed that she was weatherly but if two-deckers like *Dublin* and *Dragon* were superior to windward then it was, at best, a relative quality. The main problem was the tendency to lee helm, a dangerous feature in a sailing ship, since in certain circumstances falling off the wind would make her vulnerable to broaching or dismasting. This was undoubtedly a result of the unbalanced ketch rig, with insufficient aftersail on the mizzen to drive the hull up into the wind, the large main – positioned forward of amidships – having a disproportionate turning moment off the wind. She was, however, a stiff sailer, but although there is little reference to her rolling to any degree the large reserve of stability that this implies may have made this class lively gun platforms.

How the stepping of the masts was arranged in the ship rigged vessels is clear from the draughts. The fore mast was steeped right forward, the main just abaft amidships, and the mizzen just before the wheel on the quarterdeck. When looked at against the typical ship rigged sloop of the day the positions of the masts were not dissimilar. Whilst this had benefits for the sailing qualities, it did not solve the problem of 'wooding' (masking the arc of fire of a gun), particularly for the after mortar. The bed of this mortar is just abaft of the main mast and the main channels are placed on top of the gunwales. Even allowing for normal practice – striking some of the running rigging when in action – this must have been a serious handicap. The forward mortar does not appear to suffer to quite the same degree.

With the coming of the ship rig to some, if not all, of the bomb vessels, they took another step toward the mainstream of small cruiser design, although in terms of appearance they could still be distinguished from their ship rigged sloop cousins. The question might be asked about the wisdom of devoting so much time and effort to developing a specialist form such as the bomb vessel, given the problems they seem to have suffered to date. Unfortunately no evidence has come to light as to whether such a debate did occur. Although the continued development of the bomb over the next fifty years would lean to the conclusion that if such questions were asked the perceived advantages of the specialist vessel won the day.

Once in service some of the problems which had recurred since the earliest bomb vessels were again manifest. The *Carcass* for example as early as July 1759 was the subject of correspondence between the captain and the Navy Board, the purport of which was that the straining of the decks was causing them to leak, much akin to letters from captains of bombs in the 1740s quoted in an earlier chapter.[81] In fact the subject of the strain to the decks and hulls of these vessel is a *leitmotif* running throughout their careers. One of her predecessors, the *Furnace*, had other problems not inconsistent with the types of strain put on the hull of a bomb by both the dead weight of the mortar and the effects of their firing. In April 1759 the captain reported to the officers of Portsmouth yard, 'That in bad weather she makes three feet of water in a watch'.[82]

The remedy proposed was 'Trying her butts and seams, and after her bottom is caulked, and the old nail holes spiled up to sheath her again.'[83] With shells and carcasses stowed low down in the vessel in the bomb room the fact that she was making so much water, albeit in heavy weather, must of been a cause for concern. The *Furnace* had seen hard service, being used as an exploration vessel, but the strains of that and her previous service seemed to be telling on her by 1759 – which raises yet another question, of the life expectancy of these vessels given the immense strains they were subject to.

During the Seven Years War the *Infernals* were to see much service, both in home waters in descents on the Continental coast, and in foreign operations such as the attack on Morro Castle in Cuba. But the next war was to be different in both temper and how the navy responded to it.

6. *The American War of Independence*

All the previous wars of the eighteenth century had been dynastic struggles, with the great powers of Europe jockeying for relative advantage, but the conflict that came to a head with the declaration of American independence in 1776 was to be very different. To all intents and purposes it was a civil war, and the government's decision to coerce the recalcitrant colonists was not universally approved within parliament or the country. As such, the navy's role was less clearly defined than it had been in previous wars, and the application of force less rigorous.[84] In essence this was to be the first of the ideological wars, fought over political principles rather than the simple acquisition of territory or economic resources.

This had an effect on the use of the bomb vessel during the conflict, and particularly in the early stages when it was felt that the Americans might be, from the government's point of view, brought to their senses. At first the Navy was employed intercepting arms and other aid to the rebels, and it was regarded as politically unacceptable to bombard civilians, even if they were in rebellion against their lawful sovereign. However, military targets, fortifications and the like, were always fair game, and there was enough of a requirement for two repeats of the *Infernal* class to be ordered in February 1776.

Table 31: *ÆTNA*, OR *REPEAT INFERNAL* CLASS, 1776
Specification

Armament:	Mortars	Secondary	Men
Design	1 x 13in, 1 x 10in	8 x 6pdr, 14 swivels	60
As completed	1 x 13in, 1 x 10in	8 x 6pdr, 14 swivels	
When fitted as sloops		14 x 6pd, 14 swivels	110

	Gun deck ft-ins	Keel ft-ins	Breadth ft-ins	Depth in hold ft-ins	Burthen tons
Design	91-6	74-1¼	27-6	12-1	298²²/₉₄
As completed					
Ætna	91-9½	74-5	27-8	12-1	303
Vesuvius	91-6	74-2	27-8	12-1	302
Terror	92-1	74-7	27-10	12-0	307
Thunder	92-0	74-4¼	27-9	12-0¼	305

Building data

Name	Ordered	Builder	Laid down	Launched	Fate
Ætna	14 Feb 1776	Randall	Mar 1776	20 Jun 1776	BU 1784
Vesuvius	14 Feb 1776	Perry	Mar 1776	3 Jul 1776	Sold 1812
Terror	13 Nov 1778	Randall	Dec 1778	2 Jun 1779	Sold 1812
Thunder	13 Nov 1778	Randall	Dec 1778	18 May 79	Foundered 1781

Of the seven which had been built to the design in the 1750s only the *Carcass* survived to see service in the American War of Independence. All the rest had either been sold, or in the case of the *Basilisk* captured. Four of the six which had survived were sold as late as 1774. From the small amount of expenditure devoted to them, as quoted in the previous chapter, it is easy to see why. With the exception of the *Carcass*, converted for exploration work, from the 1760s until approximately 1772 very little maintenance was carried out: amounts in tens of pounds can represent little more than an inspection by the dockyard officers, after which they were ordered to be sold. Thus an asset which had cost nearly £4500 to build and fit out was allowed to waste away and when war came it became necessary to build anew.

Besides the two ordered in 1776, a further pair was laid down after the French entry into the war in 1778. However, their employment was restricted, because bomb vessels were slow, unhandy and vulnerable and could only be safely sent into action in situations where sea control was assured. After France and Spain entered the war, the Royal Navy was outnumbered and Britain could not guarantee command of the sea in any theatre for very long.

In terms of ship design there was to be no significant movement forward over the *Infernals*, but here was a design which would see service until 1812.

Given that the basic design did not change it is interesting to look at the sailing reports which survive for two of the four vessels built at this time. Table 32 sets out the report for the *Vesuvius* and Table 33 for the *Ætna*.

Table 32: SAILING QUALITIES OF THE *VESUVIUS*[85]
9 July 1781

Her best sailing draught of water, when victualled and stored for Channel service 13ft 3in afore, 12ft 3in aft, or as much lighter (at the same difference) as she is able to bear sail. Her lowest gundeck ports will then be above the surface of the water 4ft 11in, after port —, fore ditto —.

Query the first. How she behaves close-hauled and how many knots she runs:

In a topgallant gale 5½kts in smooth water

In a topsail gale 4kts

How she steers, and how she wears and stays steers and wears very well, carries a very slack helm if there is a sea, therefore unsure in stays

Under her reefed topsails never tried

reefed courses never tried

And query, whether she will stay under her courses never tried

Query the 2nd. In each circumstance above mentioned (in sailing with other ships) in what proportion she gathers to windward, and in what proportion she forereaches, and in general her proportion of leeway forereaches as much as most ships but very leewardly blowing fresh if the water is not smooth

Query the 3rd. How she proves in sailing through all variations of the wind ... in every strength of gale... and how many knots she runs ... and how she carries her helm wind abaft the beam 8 or 9kts and steers very well

Query the 4th. The most knots she runs before the wind, and how she rolls in the trough of the sea 8kts rolls very deep

Query the 5th. How she behaves lying too under a main sail and also under a mizzen balanced lays to very well under balanced mizzen; never tried her under main sail

Query the 6th. What for a roader she is [How she rides at anchor] and how she careens a good roader; never careened

....

Query the 10th. The trim of the ship [no data]

Table 33: SAILING QUALITIES OF THE *ÆTNA*[86]
23 April 1782

Her best sailing draught of water, when victualled and stored for Channel service — afore, — aft, or as much lighter (at the same difference) as she is able to bear sail. Her lowest gundeck ports will then be above the surface of the water —, after port —, fore ditto —.

Query the first. How she behaves close-hauled and how many knots she runs:

In a topgallant gale about 3kts, steers easy, will stay in smooth water

In a topsail gale about 3½kts

How she steers, and how she wears and stays [no data]

Under her reefed topsails 2kts, steers easy, very often misses stays with a head sea and will not stay without a mizzen

reefed courses [no data]

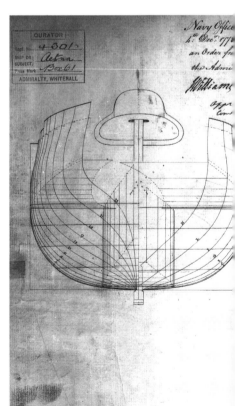

Ætna, 1776, design lines and profile.

As repeats of the *Infernal* class there was not a huge difference between these vessels and their earlier sisters. All of the class built in the 1770s were ship rigged, although the main mast was moved from between the bomb beds to abaft both, making for a better balanced sail plan. The resulting position of the channels and deadeyes meant that the mortars were not restricted in the same way. The midship section shows very clearly that although purpose-built they were not far removed from their merchant vessel cousins in hull form.

And query, whether she will stay under her courses will not stay under courses, wears very well

Query the 2nd. In each circumstance above mentioned (in sailing with other ships) in what proportion she gathers to windward, and in what proportion she forereaches, and in general her proportion of leeway in sailing with other ships is very leewardly, seldom forereaches with loaded merchant ships

Query the 3rd. How she proves in sailing through all variations of the wind ... in every strength of gale... and how many knots she runs.. and how she carries her helm with the wind abaft the beam sails very well, but on a bowline with a head sea and a stiff sea very indifferent; carries her helm amidships

Query the 4th. The most knots she runs before the wind, and how she rolls in the trough of the sea 8kts rolls easy

Query the 5th. How she behaves lying too under a main sail and also under a mizzen balanced lays to very well

Query the 6th. What for a roader she is [How she rides at anchor] and how she careens a very good roader; careens easy

....

Query the 10th. The trim of the ship best draught 12ft 0in afore, abaft 12ft 2in

Neither of these vessels was very fast – indeed, they were significantly slower than the earlier ketch rigged *Thunder* – and if *Ætna* could not keep up with laden merchantmen then it suggests that the ship was badly out of trim. The *Ætna* seems to have manifested some of the problems seen in earlier bomb vessels, such as missing stays in anything but a smooth

sea, so the switch to ship rig was not a total solution. Whilst the sailing reports are instructive, especially when looked at against that for the *Thunder* given in the previous chapter, it is clear that the basic design of the bomb did not advance during this period. The fact that for the first four years of the war it was still seen as a rebellion did have an effect on naval policy and hence the restricted opportunity to employ bombs in action. However, the entry of France and Spain into the conflict potentially changed the situation, although in practice loss of sea control by the British prohibited the kind of strategy seen in the previous war. In these circumstances there was little incentive to develop the bomb vessel beyond its mid-century design plateau. The next major step in bomb vessel development was not taken until the dawn of the new century.

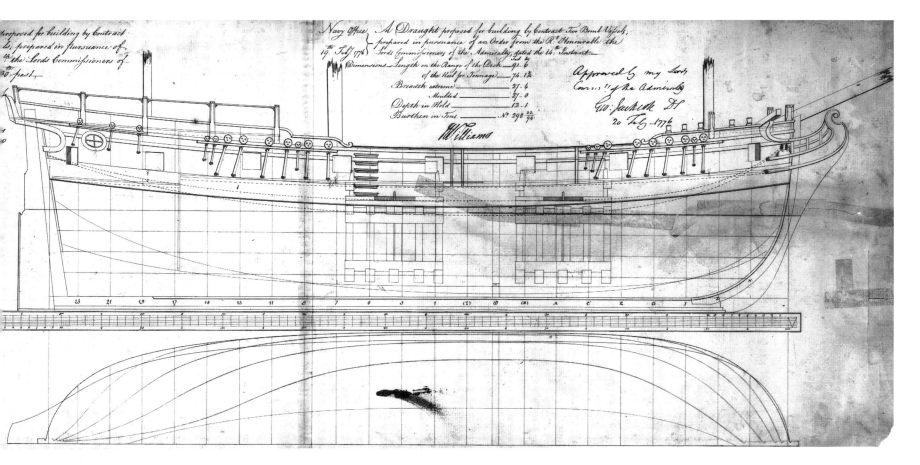

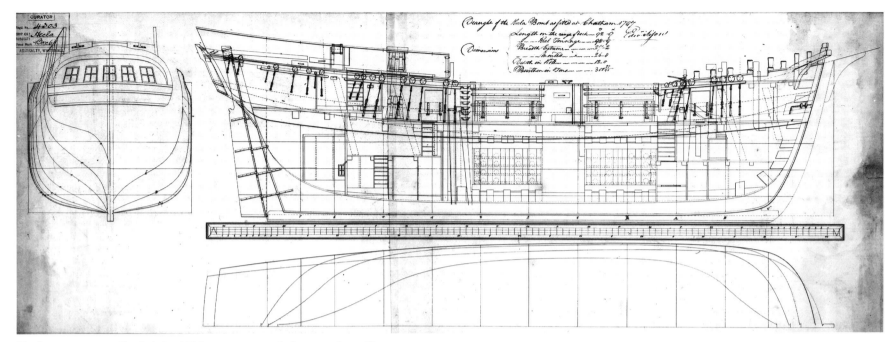

Hecla, ex-mercantile *Scipio*, 1797, as converted sheer and profile.

Seven merchant ships were taken up for conversion to bomb vessels in April 1797, all being fitted for the novel feature of low angle fire. This involved elaborate folding bulwarks – in this draught masking the mortars themselves – and blast-proof embrasures to allow the mortars to fire across the deck without damage.

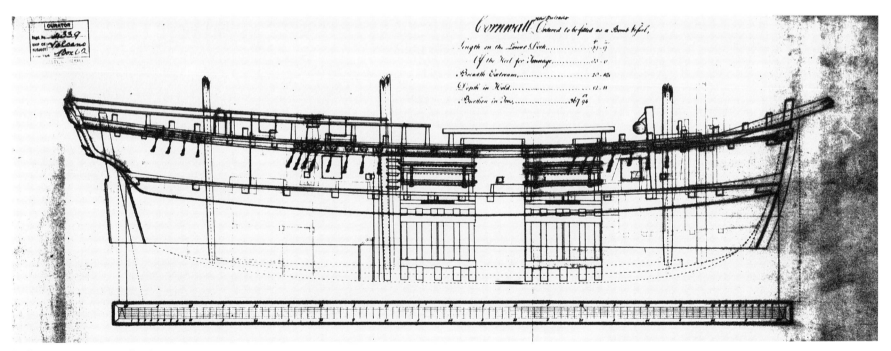

Volcano, ex-mercantile *Cornwall*, 1797, as converted sheer and profile.

Another of the 1797 conversions, *Volcano* was fitted in a similar fashion to *Hecla*.

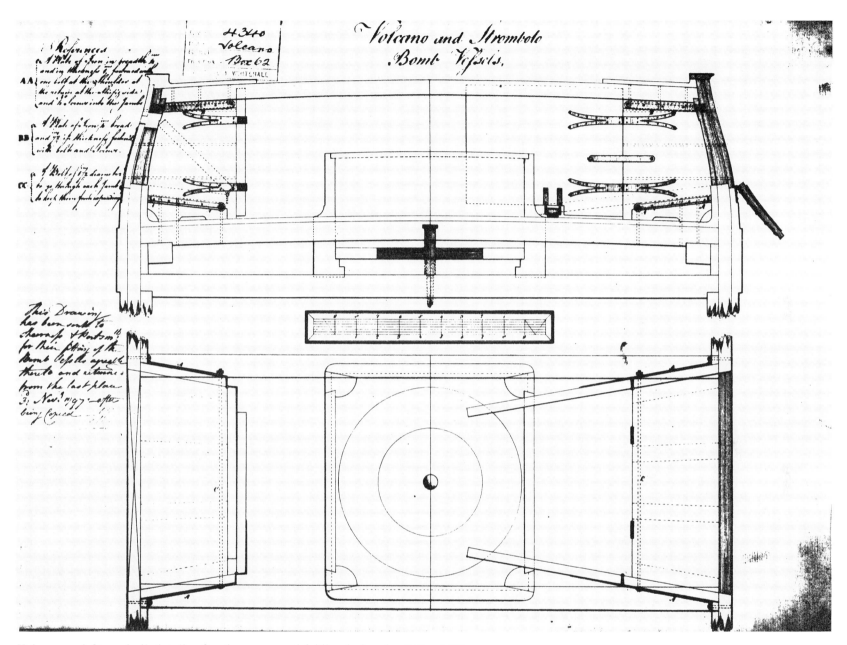

Volcano and *Stromboli*, details of embrasures and folding bulwarks, 3 Nov 1797.

Although only two vessels are mentioned, essentially similar fittings seem to have been applied to all the 1797 conversions. Not only do the bulwarks open outwards but to prepare for action the embrasures are assembled from a fold-down sloping floor and hinged two-piece sidewalls, shown closed on the left and open on the right of this sketch.

7. The Great War, 1793-1815

THE NEW AMERICAN STATE gained its independence in 1783 and Britain made peace with France and Spain. However, during the short peace that ensued, much of the European political landscape changed. The Revolution in France sent shock waves through the monarchies in the rest of Europe, and when the inevitable war followed it was to be on a new scale, in which all of the combatant nations' resources were mobilised on a scale never before experienced. The Revolutionary and Napoleonic Wars have been called by some the first true world war, and for those that survived the epic struggle it was often referred to as the

Great War. Although the strategy altered as the war progressed, in essence British economic and industrial power, defended by the Royal Navy, was pitted against French military might in a classic sea power versus land power confrontation. For much of the period, France could not defeat or circumvent British naval dominance, but Britain could not intervene decisively on the continent. The traditional policy of subsidising allies while attacking French colonies was employed for some time, but political necessity often required diversions on the continent, while the threat of invasion also led to bombardments of concentrations of shipping in Channel ports. As a result both the bomb vessel and the fireship were to see a massive resurgence in their use and development.

Of the four vessels purpose built in the preceding war only two survived into the Revolutionary war – *Vesuvius* and *Terror*. Thus by the outbreak of war the design was thirty-six years old. In terms of the norm for other wooden warships this would seem unsurprising, but it does emphasise the basic soundness of the *Infernal* design. As an interim solution the Admiralty resorted to the policy of a century before, purchasing merchant vessels and converting older naval vessels to fill the gap. Table 34 lists merchant vessels purchased into the service in the 1790s.

The *Explosion, Hecla, Strombolo, Sulphur, Tartarus,* and *Volcano* were purchased in April of 1797, and whilst they were not purpose built for the job they do nonetheless have some novel features. In the case of the *Hecla* this was the fact that her bulwarks in the way of the bomb beds were made to hinge so that they could be cleared away when firing was

Table 34: PURCHASED BOMBS 1797-1802
Specification

Armament:	Mortars	Secondary				Men
Design						
As completed						
Explosion	2 x 10in	4 x 6pdr, 6 x 18pdr carr				67
Hecla	2 x 10in	4 x 6pdr, 6 x 18pdr carr				67
Strombolo	2 x 10in	4 x 6pdr, 6 x 18pdr carr				67
Sulphur	2 x 10in	4 x 6pdr, 6 x 18pdr carr				67
Tartarus	2 x 10in	4 x 6pdr, 6 x 18pdr carr				67
Volcano	2 x 10in	4 x 6pdr, 6 x 18pdr carr				67
Thunder	2 x 10in?	?				?
	Gun deck ft-ins	Keel ft-ins	Breadth ft-ins	Depth in hold ft-ins	Burthen tons	
Design						
As completed						
Explosion	96-4	80-4½	27-6	12-9	323²⁹/₉₄	
Hecla	92-9	76-5	27-2	12-5	300	
Strombolo	92-5	75-2	29-0¼	12-6½	323⁶⁴/₉₄	
Sulphur	96-10¼	79-3½	29-0	13-0	354⁶¹/₉₄	
Tartarus	94-6	79-10	28-6	12-2	344²⁶/₉₄	
Volcano	99-9	83-0	28-10½	12-11	367⁵²/₉₄	
Thunder					230	

Building data

Name	Previous name	When purchased	Fate
Explosion	*Gloucester*	Apr 1797	Wrecked off Heligoland 10 Sep 1807
Hecla	*Scipio*	Apr 1797	BU 1813
Strombolo	*Leander*	Apr 1797	BU 1809
Sulphur	*Severn*	Apr 1797	Hulked 1805, sold 1816
Tartarus	*Charles Jackson*	Apr 1797	Wrecked Margate Sands 1804
Volcano	*Cornwall*	Apr 1797	Sold 1810
Thunder	*Die Guter Erwatung*	Apr 1797	Sold 1802

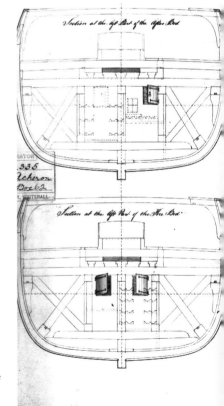

Acheron, 1804, as fitted profile and section.

As discussed in the text, resort was had to conversion of merchant vessels, both in the seventeenth and eighteenth centuries. The *Acheron* was one of the group converted in 1804. The section shows the heavy supports which were necessary for the mortar beds. The midship sections of the *Acheron* and the *Infernal*, whilst not congruent, betray a common ancestry.

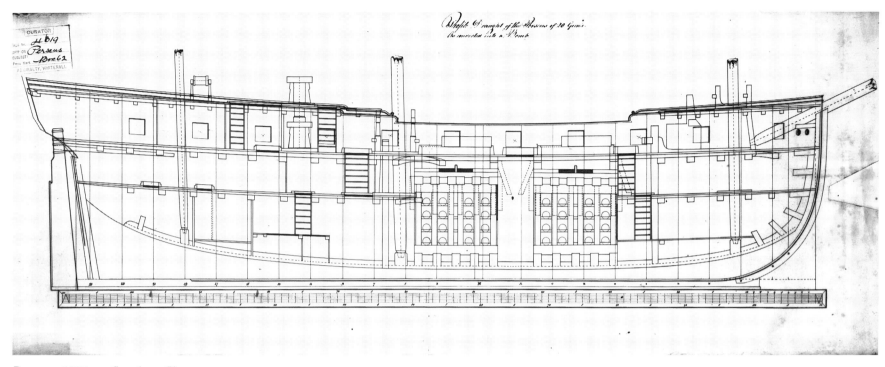

Perseus, 1776, as fitted profile.

The *Perseus* was one of a group of merchant and small warships converted to bomb vessels in the French Revolutionary War. The bomb beds cut through the lower decks, although as with all bomb vessels the bomb beds and their supports could be removed. In hull form she is closer to the later *Vesuvius* class than her predecessors the *Infernal*s. Like the *Vesuvius* class she carries a double capstan.

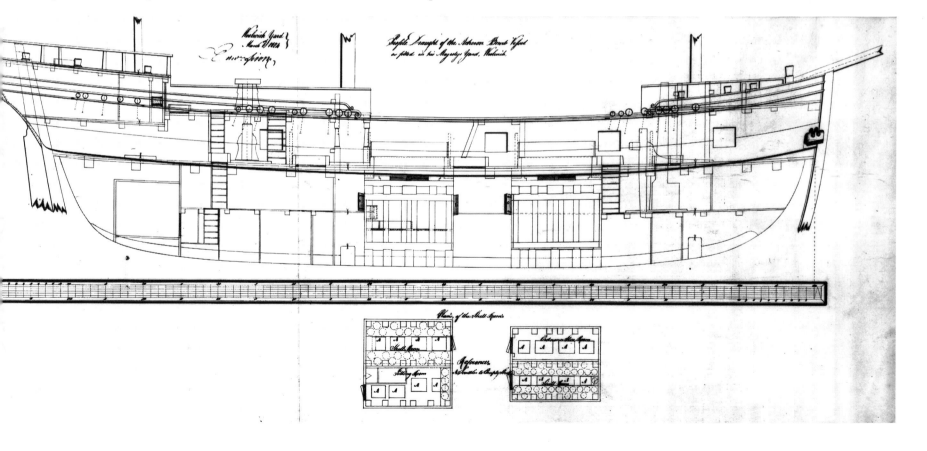

Table 35: WARSHIPS CONVERTED TO BOMBS, 1797-1802
Specification

Armament:	Mortars		Secondary		Men
Design					
As completed					
Discovery	1 x 13in,? 1 x 10in?		?		
Perseus	1 x 13in, 1 x 10in		10 x 6pdr		
Zebra	1 x 13in,? 1 x 10in?		?		
Bulldog	1 x 13in,? 1 x 10 in		?		
Fury	1 x 13in, 1 x 10in?		10 x 6pdr, 12 swivels		

	Gun deck ft-ins	Keel ft-ins	Breadth ft-ins	Depth in hold ft-ins	Burthen tons
Design					
As completed					
Discovery	99-2	77-9⅝	28-3¼		330⁶⁵/₉₄
Perseus	108-0	89-8	30-0	9-8	429²³/₉₄
Zebra	98-0	80-1¼	27-2	13-4	314⁴²/₉₄
Bulldog	98-0	80-1¼	27-1	13-4	314⁴²/₉₄
Fury	100-0	82-9¾	27-0	13-0	320⁸⁹/₉₄

Building data

Name	Ordered	Builder	Laid down	Launched	Fitted as bomb	Fate
Discovery		Randall, Rotherhithe		1789	1798	Hulked 1808, BU 1834
Perseus	30 Oct 1775	Randall, Rotherhithe	Nov 1775	20 Apr 1776	1798	BU 1805
Bulldog		Ladd, Dover	Oct 1782	10 11 1782	1798	Hulked 1801
Fury	17 Jan 1778	Portsmouth Dyd	Jul 1788	2 Mar 1790	1798	BU 1811
Zebra	16 Sep 1779	Cleverley, Gravesend	Oct 1779	31 Aug 1780	1798	Sold 1812

in progress. The intention seems to have been to allow firing at lower angles of elevation, but the reason why this was thought potentially useful is unclear. The other novelty was the harmonising of the main armament of all of the vessels taken into service in 1797. In terms of defensive armament they no longer carried the long 4pdr or 6pdr but were fitted with a variety of carronades. This in some way was ideal as the shorter barrel length was better suited to the confined deck space. In term of rig all carried the three-masted square (ship) rig. In the *Hecla* the channels were set on the forecastle and right aft on the poop, an arangement made necessary by the hinged bulwark system alluded to earlier.

In this same period five naval vessels were converted – although strictly speaking only four from warships – to serve as bombs; they are listed in Table 35. This was an heterogeneous group, ranging from a merchant vessel originally purchased on the stocks and converted to Vancouver's

exploration vessel, the *Discovery*, to ship sloops in the case of the *Zebra*, *Bulldog* and *Fury*, built in 1780, 1782 and 1790 respectively; the *Perseus* had been a small Sixth Rate of 24 guns. There is a surviving sailing report for the *Discovery* for the period when she was a bomb, and in the case of the *Perseus* there is a specification for her conversion. These documents allow us some idea of what was involved in the process of conversion and how the naval vessels performed once they had been converted. Table 36 gives the details of the sailing quality report for the *Discovery*.

Table 36: SAILING QUALITIES OF THE *DISCOVERY*[88]
1st November 1801

Her best sailing draught of water, when victualled and stored for Channel service 15ft 6in **afore**, 15ft 8in **aft**, or as much lighter (at the same difference) as she is able to bear sail. Her lowest gundeck ports will then be above the surface of the water —, after port —, fore ditto —.

Query the first. How she behaves close-hauled and how many knots she runs:

In a topgallant gale 5kts

In a topsail gale 6kts

How she steers, and how she wears and stays steers indifferent, wears and stays very well

Under her reefed topsails 3kts reefed courses 2kts

And query, whether she will stay under her courses she will stay under courses

Query the 2nd. In each circumstance above mentioned (in sailing with other ships) in what proportion she gathers to windward, and in what proportion she forereaches, and in general her proportion of leeway seldom forereaches on any ship, from 1 point to 2½ leeway

Query the 3rd. How she proves in sailing through all variations of the wind ... in every strength of gale... and how many knots she runs ... and how she carries her helm improved by sailing two points free, close hauled with a head sea she sails very bad, weather helm

Query the 4th. The most knots she runs before the wind, and how she rolls in the trough of the sea 9kts rolls very much

Query the 5th. How she behaves lying too under a main sail and also under a mizzen balanced never tried

Query the 6th. What for a roader she is [How she rides at anchor] and how she careens very good roader; careen never tried

....

Query the 10th. The trim of the ship best draught 15ft 6in afore, abaft 15ft 8in, height of gundeck above water 7ft, nearly even keel

The *Discovery* was slightly larger in overall dimensions than some previous bombs or bomb conversions. As an ex-transport/exploration ship she was built for capacity rather than speed – noticeable in the larger than usual draught – although she could manage 9kts before the wind, albeit that she rolled very heavily, another characteristic she shared with many of her purpose-built cousins. Another theme which runs through-out the development of the bomb is the problem of heavy rolling. Many of the reports already quoted in previous chapters mention 'deep and heavy rolling' or 'rolls very much'. Even allowing for these terms not being

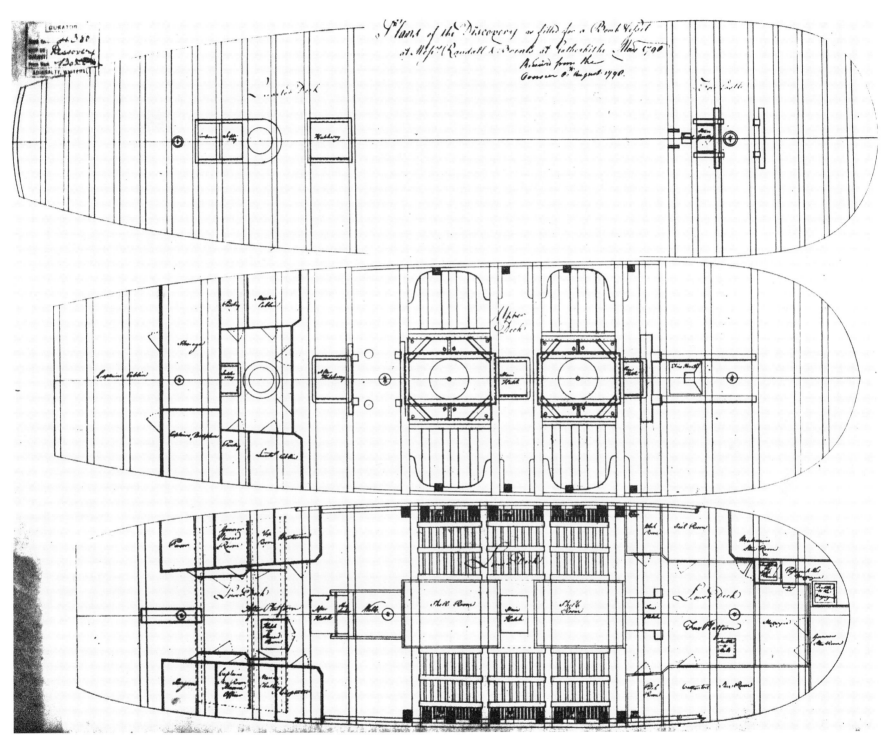

Discovery, **decks as converted to a bomb, 1798.**

More famous as the ship in which Vancouver made his voyages of exploration, the vessel was a typically deep-hulled merchantman purchased while building. She was later converted to a bomb vessel, but unlike the earlier conversions of 1797 the later vessels eschewed the complicated embrasures and folding bulwarks, low-angle fire having proved unnecessary or impractical in action.

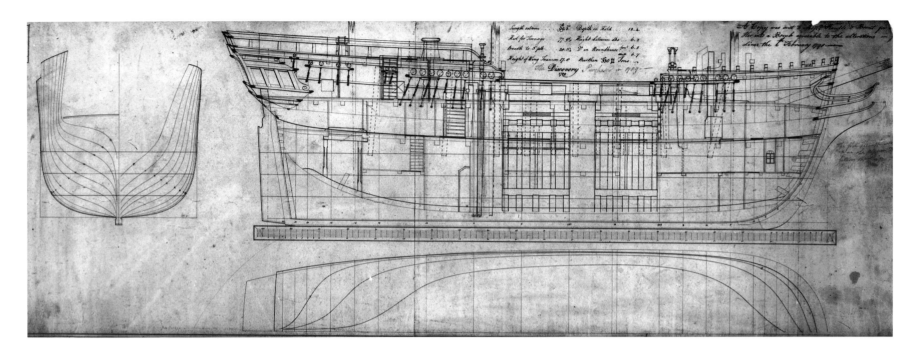

Discovery, **sheer and profile as converted to a bomb, 1798.**

The depth of the hull is apparent, as is the typically full mercantile section, but the flared topsides were not at all common at a time when most ships still showed some tumblehome above the waterline.

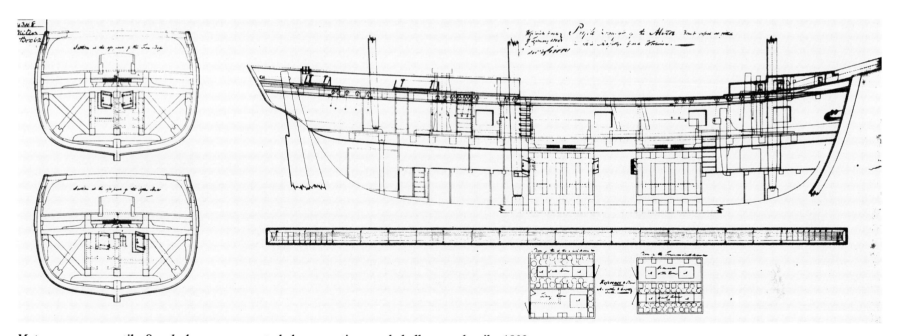

Meteor, **ex-mercantile** *Sarah Ann,* **as converted sheer, sections and shell room details, 1803.**

The elaborate fittings of the 1797 conversions were obviously a design cul de sac and later vessels reverted to simpler fittings. Note the diagonal cross-bracing in the hold.

Table 37: CONVERTED BOMBS, AFTER 1803
(a) Purchased merchant vessels, 1803
Specification

Armament:	Mortars	Secondary	Men
Design			
As completed			
Meteor	1 x 13in, 1 x 10in	8 x 24pdr carr	67
Acheron	1 x 13in, 1 x 10in	8 x 24pdr carr	67
Devastation	1 x 13in, 1 x 10in	8 x 24pdr carr	67
Ætna	1 x 13in, 1 x 10in	8 x 24pdr carr	67
Lucifer	1 x 13in, 1 x 10in	8 x 24pdr carr	67
Prospero	1 x 13in, 1 x 10in	8 x 24pdr carr	67
Thunder	1 x 13in, 1 x 10in	8 x 24pdr carr	67

	Gun deck ft-ins	Keel ft-ins	Breadth ft-ins	Depth in hold ft-ins	Burthen tons
Design					
As completed					
Meteor	102-6	80-0	29-3	12-11	364
Acheron	108-3	85-9	29-2	12-9	388
Devastation	108-5	85-9	29-2	12-9	388
Ætna	102-0	81-0	29-2½	12-6	368
Lucifer	110-0	87-9	29-2	13-0	397
Prospero	107-0	87-0	30-5	13-6	400
Thunder	95-0	75-10	28-1		318

Building data

Name	Previous name	Builder	Purchased	Fitted as bomb	Fate
Meteor	*Sarah Ann*	Newcastle	Oct 1803	1803	Sold 1811
Acheron	*New Grove*	Whitby	Oct 1803	1803	Taken and burnt by the French 3 Feb 1805
Devastation	*Intrepid*		Oct 1803	1803	
Ætna	*Success*		Oct 1803	1803	Sold 1816
Lucifer	*Spring*		Oct 1803	1803	Sold 1811
Prospero	*Albion*		Oct 1803	1803	Foundered off Dieppe 18 Feb 1807
Thunder	*Dasher*		Oct 1803	1803	Sold 1814

(b) Warships converted to bombs, 1803-16
Specification

Armament:	Mortars	Secondary	Men
Design			
As completed			
Hound	1 x 13in, 1 x 10in	10 x 24pdr carr	67
Proselyte	1 x 13in, 1 x 10in	6 x 24pdr and 2 x 18pdr carr	70
Strombolo	?	?	?
Heron	?	?	?
Meteor	?	?	?

	Gun deck ft-ins	Keel ft-ins	Breadth ft-ins	Depth in hold ft-ins	Burthen tons
Design					
As completed					
Hound	103-3	81-0	27-9½		333
Proselyte	107-6	87-3¼	29-6		404
Strombolo	98-11	78-6	28-4		335
Heron	97-6		29-0		339
Meteor	106-0	87-7	28-0	13-9	365

Building data

Name	Ordered	Builder	Laid down	Purchased	Fitted as bomb	Fate
Hound				Feb 1801	1807	BU 1812
Proselyte		North Shields		1804	1808	Wrecked on Anholt Reef 5 Dec 1808
Strombolo		South Shields		28 Feb 1800	1810	Sold 1815
Heron		Newcastle	Jun 1804	1811		Sold 1816
Meteor	27 Nov 1802	Tanner, Dartmouth		26 Jul 1805	1812	Sold 1816

Notes: Hound was an purchased sloop, *Proselyte* a purchased Sixth Rate converted, *Strombolo* was ex-*Autumn* a purchased sloop, *Heron* was a purchased sloop converted and the *Meteor* was ex-*Star*, a *Merlin* class ship sloop converted.

scientific it would appear to point up the difficulty of combining a capacious hull, necessary to carry the weight of the mortars, with lines that made the ship a reasonable performer under sail. Some of the earlier vessels, with relatively fine-lined sloop-like hulls, inevitably rolled deeply, but even the deep, square-sectioned *Discovery* suffered equally.

In term of conversion the specification for the *Perseus* is instructive:[89] to bear the weight the ship was 'To have five futtock riders of oak under each mortar .... Beams under the mortars – to have double beams under the centre of each mortar bed, sided together at 2 foot and moulded 13 inches'. Two more beams were to be placed under each bed, again of 13in moulded dimension. All of this was to be fixed with bolts $1^{1}/_{8}$in in

diameter. To support this there were eighteen pillars, six under each centre beam and three each under the other beams. All of these pillars were to be so constructed that they could be 'Taken down and put up again'.[90]

The bomb room was to be 8ft by 10ft and to be enclosed with a thick coaming as high as the deck. The bomb room and its supports were to be constructed so that the room itself was resistant to the firing of the mortar. There were to be hatch covers to protect the mortars when not in use and ringbolts fixed inside the mortar pit to help with their traversing. The whole impression from this document is of a very massive amount of reinforcement to transfer the strain of carrying and firing the mortars to the hull, but also one which could be revised if need be.

This conversion was literally building on a century of experience with the bomb. However the design of the vessels was not fundamentally

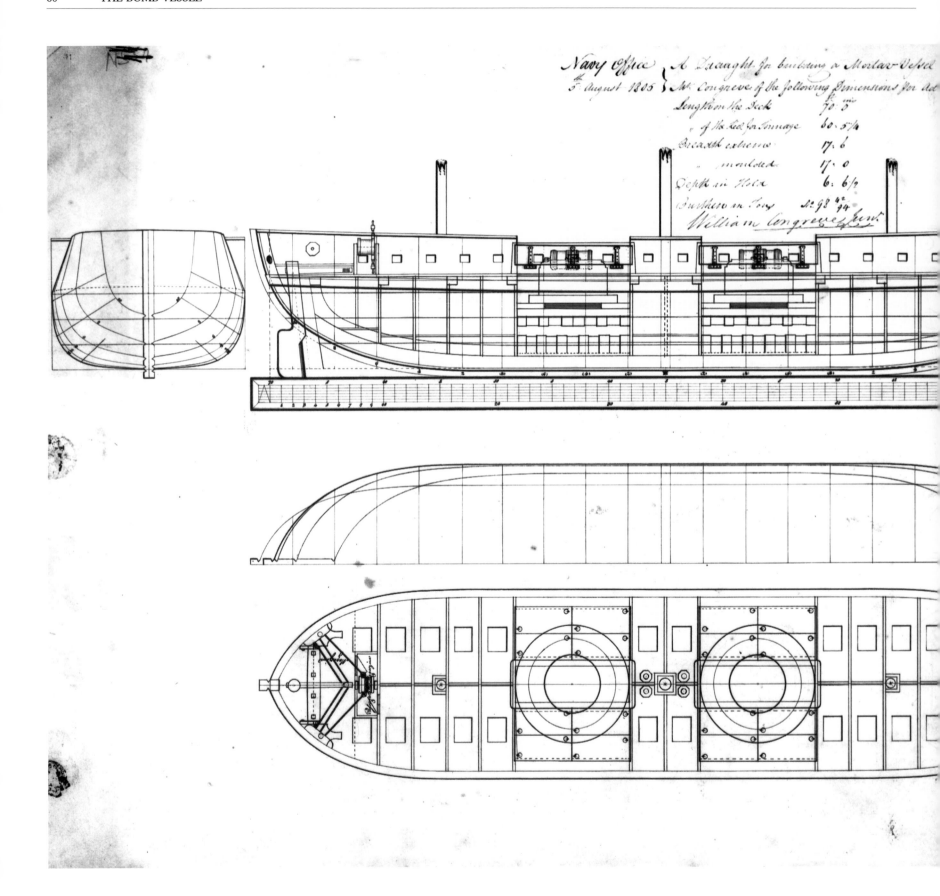

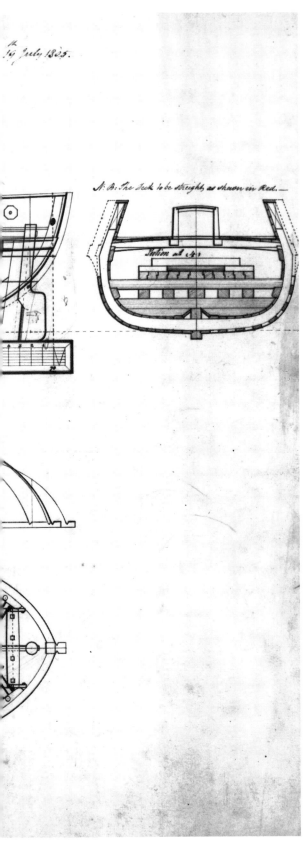

Project, 1805, **design hull plan and section.**

This plan show quite clearly the experimental nature of the *Project*. The double rudder is visible at bow and stern as are the twin helm positions. Her lack of depth and flat bottom must have made her an uncomfortable sailer.

changed by the work carried out on the *Perseus*. What had been done to the *Hecla* was an innovation, and there is evidence that it was also applied to at least one purpose-built bomb. The *Vesuvius* of 1776 had been fitted with similar 'embrasures' (the term was taken from fortification where it indicated a funnel-shaped gunport in a wall or bastion), but in 1808 it was decided that since the mortars had not been fired at low angle, and the ironwork of the folding 'ports' was corroded, it would be better to remove the feature and revert to lighter solid built-up bulwarks.[91]

The next design changes were to come in the second phase of the war, in fact they were to come almost at the end of the war in Europe.

THE NAPOLEONIC PERIOD

With the outbreak of hostilities in 1803 after the short Peace of Amiens, to put bomb vessels into service the Admiralty at first had resort to purchase and conversion rather than to building new ships. Table 37 sets out both the mercantile and naval conversions of this period.

The first group were straight purchases from the merchant service and seem, at least in terms of fitting out, to have been treated in the same fashion. All seven carried eight 24pdr carronades and the standard fit of mortars. The second group were converted from a variety of other craft: the *Meteor* was ex-*Star*, a sloop of the *Merlin* class; *Hound* a purchased sloop, from a purchased gun vessel (28 guns); the *Strombolo* previously the hulk *Autumn*; and the *Heron* from a purchased sloop.

There is a surviving sailing quality report on one of the mercantile conversions, the *Ætna*, dated 19 August 1815.[92] The report uses the new form introduced towards the end of the Napoleonic War which not only rearranged the questions but seems to have encouraged even more cursory answers, so it does not warrant quotation in full. However, it makes it clear that the ship was crank and leewardly, but easy in her motions, except when lying to. She was capable of 5kts close-hauled under all the sail she could carry, but only 1½kts under courses; she could manage 8½kts large, or 7½kts before the wind. Her captain's summary was: 'very crank and unsafe, more ballast seems necessary'. This is not surprising since she was then carrying only 32 tons (all iron) and 27 tons of water, although in this condition she had only 2ft 4in freeboard to her midships ports. The advantage of the mercantile hull form is to be seen in the ease with which she stowed 6 months' provisions, but the poor sailing qualities were the inevitable reverse of the coin.

A major strategic concern at this time was the threatened French invasion, to which the British responded with attacks on the assembled invasion craft; simultaneously there was a new emphasis on coastal defence, with large numbers of shallow-draught gunboats being constructed. Traditional bombs were employed in the former role, but mortars were also fitted to small craft, presumably with a view to getting them closer in to the well-defended ports of continental Europe. In this atmosphere there was a willingness to try many types of unconventional warfare, including Fulton's 'torpedoes' (to which the British reacted with righteous horror when used against themselves in the War of 1812), and one of the leading lights in the experimental movement was Colonel

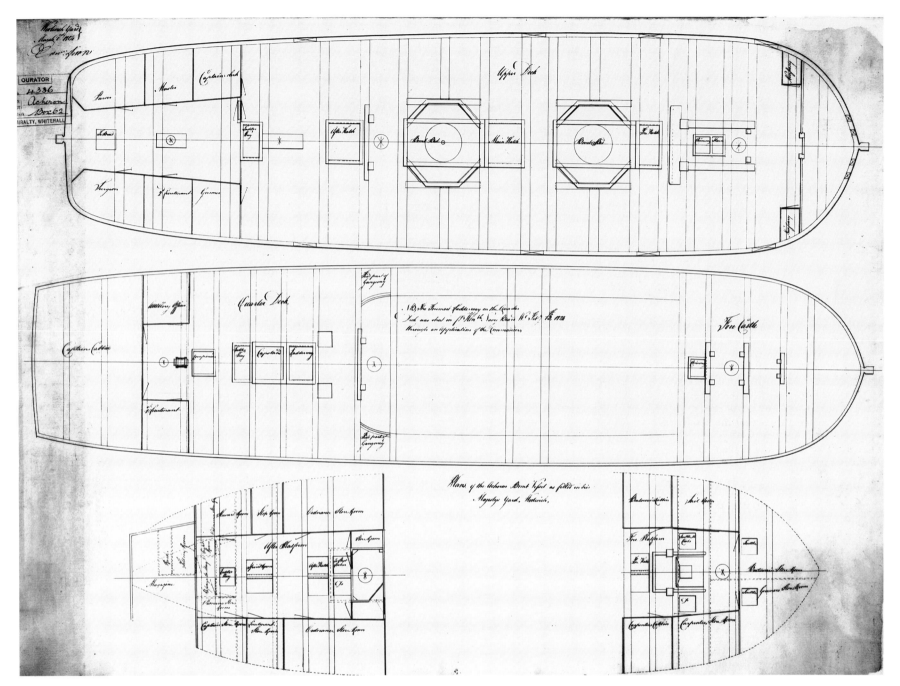

***Acheron*, 1804, as fitted deck plan.**

One of the many sets of drawings, along with the profile and section, which give a clue to the conversion of merchant vessels to bomb vessels.

William Congreve, in charge of the Royal Laboratory at Woolwich. He is best remembered for producing a viable war rocket – a device that was later to partially supersede the naval bomb – but he also designed a new type of mortar vessel.

Table 38 gives her particulars.

The barge-like hull was double-ended – to the point of having rudder and steering gear at each extremity – and carried three masts, but also had sixteen ports for oars. There is a surviving specification for this vessel which makes it clear that she was to be fitted with two 10in mortars, although the draught makes the weapons look like howitzers; the proposal is dated 19 July 1805.[93]

The beams under the mortar were to be 10in, those for the rest of the deck being 8in sided and 6½in moulded. There is no direct mention of pillars and, although there is a shell room, the depth of hold at just 6ft 6in left little room between decks. She was also to be planked in fir

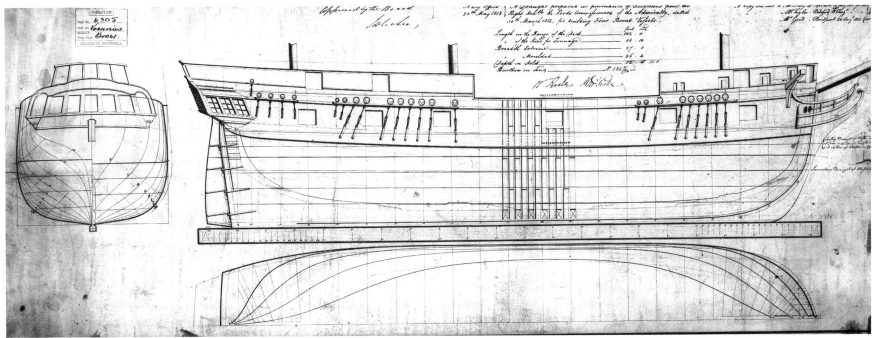

Vesuvius, 1812, design profile and section.

With the *Vesuvius* and *Hecla* class the sailing bomb vessel came to its apogee. From the profile of the vessel it is difficult to tell her apart from other minor war vessels of the period. If you compare this profile with the *Perseus* it demonstrates that the bomb vessel was being absorbed into the mainstream of ship design. Given their varied careers it is unsurprising that there are a large number of plans of *Vesuvius* and her half-sisters of the *Hecla* class.

Table 38: CONGREVE'S *PROJECT*, 1805
Specification

Armament:	Mortars		Secondary		Men
Design					
As completed	2 x 10in				

	Gun deck ft-ins	Keel ft-ins	Breadth ft-ins	Depth in hold ft-ins	Burthen tons
Design					
As completed	70-0	60-5¼	17-6	6-6½	98⁴²/₉₄

Building data

Name	Ordered	Builder	Laid down	Launched	Fate
Project	19 Jul 1805	Woolwich Dyd	Aug 1805	26 Mar 1806	BU 1810

which may help to explain why she only lasted four years in the service. Built at Woolwich Dockyard, the vessel was launched in March 1806.

Being double-ended and also of very shallow draught, her seakeeping would have been minimal, but presumably the point of the experiment was to produce a craft that could operate in confined waters where there was none of the searoom necessary for normal manoeuvres under sail; at this time there were a number of experiments with craft that could be sailed in either direction, and this seems a vessel of like ilk. The draught shows no channels so whatever the rig it must have been very light – and presumably reversible. Even the name *Project* suggests the craft was just experimental, but it shows the continuing commitment not just to the mortar but also to its wider employment.

Mortars and howitzers were also mounted in less specialised craft, and although these are outside the scope of this book they do form an interesting contrast with the traditional bomb vessels: indeed, their relative failure helps to explain the continuing need for proper bomb ships. As an example, in July 1811 a critical report on the various kinds of mortar-carrying vessels under his command by Rear-Admiral Sir Richard Keats was sent to the Board of Ordnance for their comment.[94]

Keats and the Board agreed on the poor qualities of the 'mortar brigs on the establishment of gunbrigs', but the Ordnance insisted that they had never been consulted about these craft or they would have pointed out in advance the ineffectiveness of the 8in mortars that so aggrieved the admiral. Keats preferred the 68pdr carronade, which on a high angle mounting could be very effective firing shells. He had carried out his own experiments with this weapon on the gunbrig *Fearless*, but acknowledged the experimental work done by Admiral Lord Keith when he commanded on the Downs station (effectively, the anti-invasion fleet).

By contrast admiral and Ordnance Board agreed on the efficiency

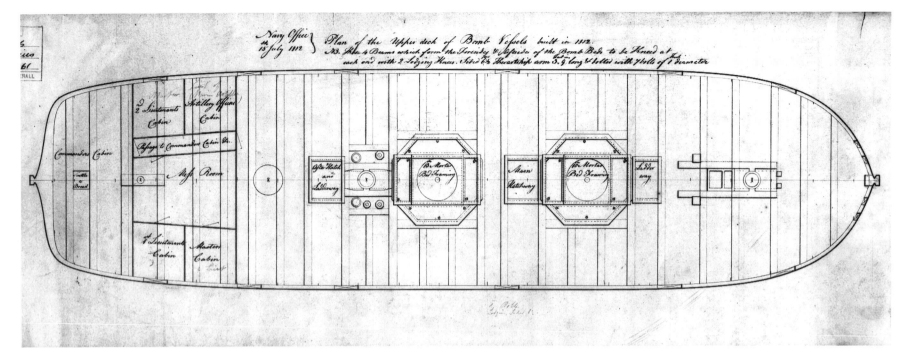

Vesuvius, 1812, design upper deck plan.

In the same way as in battleships of the steam period, the mountings for the mortars were the main openings in the hull. The main hatch is sited just aft of the fore mortar with a ladder between decks forward of it. One thing of note is that, given the changeover in 1804 from the Ordnance Board to the marines, there is accommodation for the artillery officer, next to the second lieutenant's cabin, port side.

and merits of the mortars in the 'bomb ships on the establishment of sloops of war, (*ie* conventional bomb vessels). The mortars could reach a range of 4000yds, although the fallibility of the weapons meant that prolonged firing at maximum range was inadvisable. After such a report it is not surprising that when a new shore bombardment requirement presented itself – the War of 1812 with the United States – there was recourse to the more conventional type of mortar-carrier.

Sir John Borlase Warren, commanding on the North America station requested mortars in the middle of 1812 'in case it is decided to annoy the coast of America'.[95] It already had been. In fact, the design of a new class of bombs had been ordered in March 1812, and since the draught took some months to prepare, it was probably given particular thought.[96] The resulting *Vesuvius* class, launched in 1813, was intended to be four ships but in the event only three were contracted for. This and the slightly enlarged and improved *Hecla* class, constituted the final development of the bomb in British service.

Although in topside detail the ships resembled small cruisers, in hull form they had the very full lines of a merchant ship – and the sailing qualities to match. The Admiralty was concerned that the ships should have sufficient capacity to carry their own shells, which is an interesting requirement. Such vessels had always had bomb rooms, but for long term bombardments they relied on tenders to carry a larger supply;

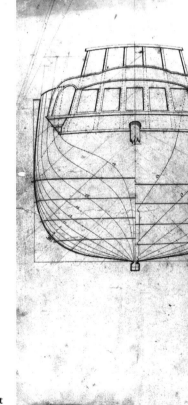

Beelzebub, 1812, design lines and profile.

The lines and profile give little away about her true use.

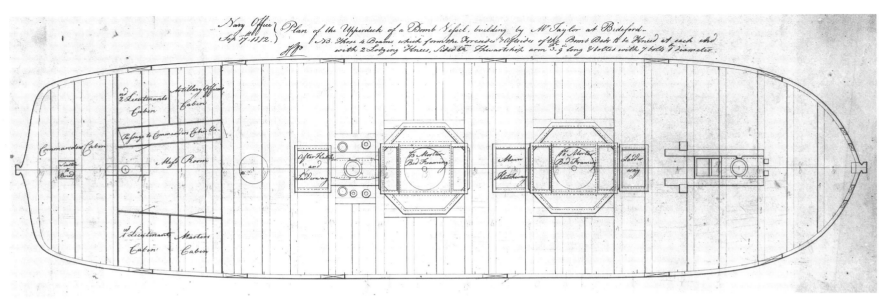

Beelzebub, 1812, design upper deck plan.

The entrance to the commander's cabin was via a passageway which separated the mess room and the second lieutenant's and artillery officer's cabins. It would appear that the master and first lieutenant had more space in their cabins but they opened into the mess room.

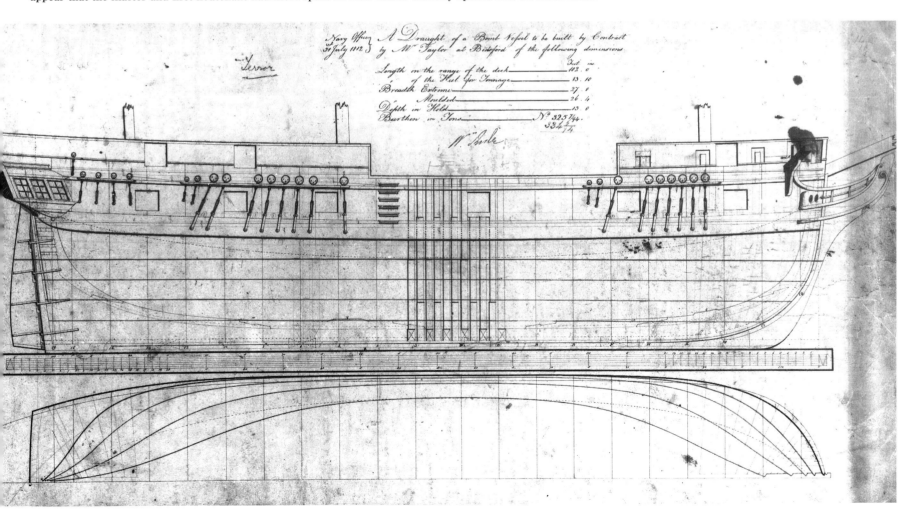

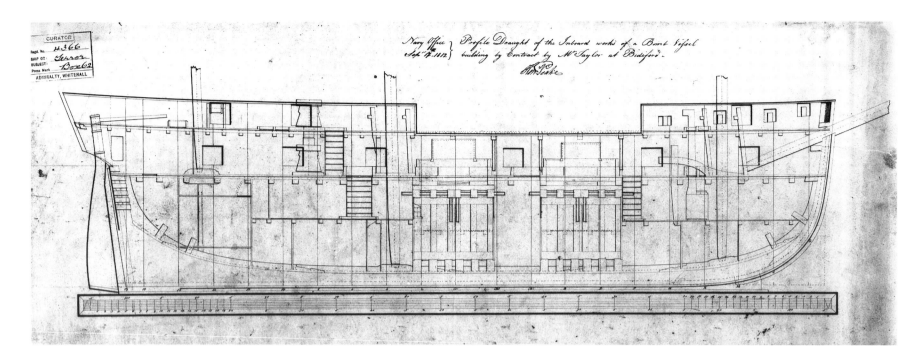

Beelzebub, 1812, design inboard profile.

Despite the stamp on the draughts Taylor built the *Beelzebub*. The double capstan is clearly visible set between the main and mizzen mast on the quarterdeck.

therefore, this class may have been designed for a degree of self-sufficiency. In one sailing quality report,[97] the captain of the *Beelzebub* gave the following breakdown of stowage necessary to get the ship to trim 1ft by the stern:

After hold	94 13in shells 200lbs each
	56 boxes small shot 110lbs each
	50 carcasses averaging 150lbs each
After cockpit	28 13in shells 200lbs each
	20 10in shells 70lbs each
	2 tons round shot
Bread room	24 13in shells 200lbs each
	20 10in shells 70lbs each
	All spare sails and slops

Beelzebub, 1812, design quarterdeck and forecastle plan.

The position of the drum helm can be made out between the two skylights on the quarterdeck. Also of note are the number of hatches in the waist of these vessels.

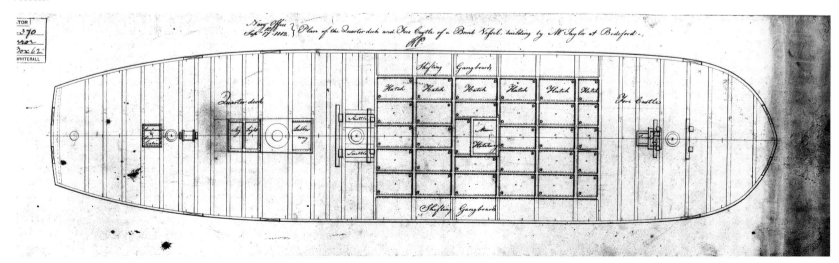

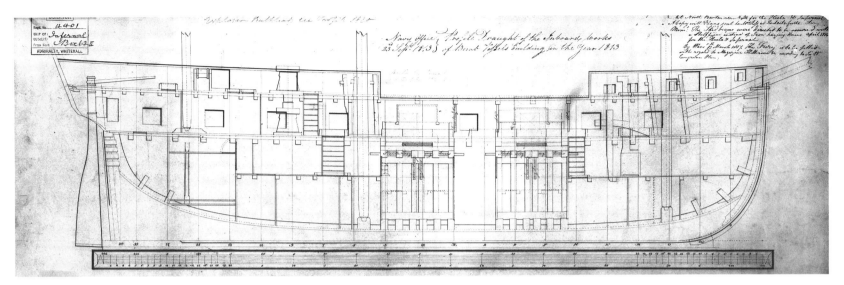

Infernal, 1815, design inboard profile.

This is the first of this class for which there is almost a full set of plans, minus only the lines and profile.

The significance of this is not so much the trim problem as the number of shells being stowed – and outside the bomb rooms.

Table 39 lists those built to the draught of the *Vesuvius* and Table 40 those of the improved *Hecla* design.

A fourth vessel, probably to have been called *Fury*, was never contracted. The *Vesuvius* was sold in 1819, the *Terror* was to find fame of a kind, being lost in the ice in 1848 on her second trip to the North Pole, and the *Beelzebub* was broken up, in 1820.

There is a sailing quality report extant for the *Beelzebub*, which suggests that the performance of this class was not much better than the mercantile conversions.[99] Speed was much the same at 5kts close-hauled and just over 9kts with the wind large or aft, and the ship was equally leewardly. Her motions were generally easy, including riding to her anchors, but she did not lie to very well. The most serious problem was that she would not carry sail at all well, basically the result of being able to stow very little ballast – 20 tons iron, plus 38 tons water gave the ship a freeboard of 4ft 6in for her gundeck ports at normal trim. The stowage of the ammunition was quoted above, but the captain also found it necessary to 'put quarterdeck and forecastle guns on the main deck, and all shot and three carronades in the hold before she would sail'; even then the main deck ports were only out of the water in a moderate breeze. The mercantile hull form of this class was obviously adopted for its capacity, but its shortcomings seem very serious, However, since the design – admittedly in modified form – continued to be used, the immediate stability problems must have been solved. Certainly in their usual peacetime employment as Polar exploration ships, there would be no particular use for speed, although power under sail might have been helpful in breaking through thinner ice floes.

The first of the *Hecla* class were ordered in 1813, suggesting a

Table 39: *VESUVIUS* CLASS, 1812[98]
Specification

Armament:	Mortars		Secondary		Men
Design					
As completed	1 x 13in, 1 x 10in		2 x 6pdr plus 8 x 24pdr carr		67

	Gun deck ft-ins	Keel ft-ins	Breadth ft-ins	Depth in hold ft-ins	Burthen tons
Design	102-0	83-10	27-0	12-6	325⁷/₉₄
As completed					
Vesuvius	102-0	83-10	27-0	12-6	325
Terror	102-4	84-2	27-3	12-11	326
Beelzebub					

Building data

Name	Ordered	Builder	Laid down	Launched	Fate
Vesuvius	30 Mar 1812	Davy, Topsham	Jul 1812	1 May 1813	Sold 1819
Terror	30 Mar 1812	Davy, Topsham	Sep 1812	29 Jun 1813	Lost 1848
Beelzebub	30 Mar 1812	Taylor, Bideford	Nov 1812	30 Jul 1813	BU 1820

decision to enlarge the *Vesuvius* design even before any had been completed. The final group was ordered as a response to a postwar report on the state of existing bombs, which led the Navy Board to ask the Admiralty in May 1819 whether present numbers were adequate – the fleet comprised *Erebus* on exploration duties, *Infernal*, *Fury* and *Beelzebub* in good condition, and *Terror* in need of a small repair. The postwar emphasis was on considered preparation for the next war, and events like the bombardment of Algiers suggested that in an emergency such vessels might be wanted inside the timescale needed to build even these small craft. After due consideration the Admiralty ordered a long term programme of replacement vessels to be built in the dockyards, five of which were launched between 1823 and 1829. Three further vessels, *Volcano*, *Vesuvius* and *Beelzebub* were cancelled with the massive

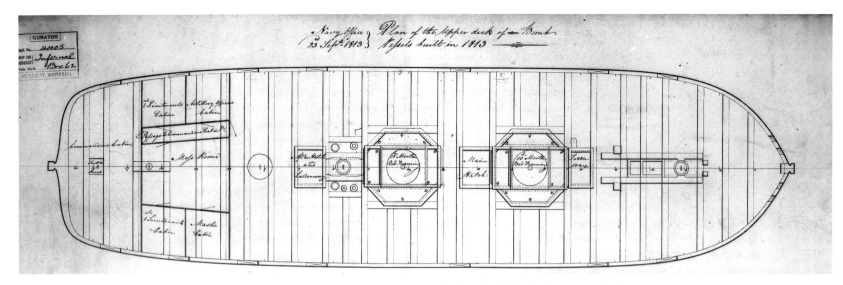

Infernal, 1815, design upper deck plan.

Table 40: *HECLA* CLASS, 1813
Specification

Armament:	Mortars		Secondary		Men
Design					
As completed	1 x 13in, 1 x 10in		2 x 6pdr plus 8 x 24pdr carr		67

	Gun deck ft-ins	Keel ft-ins	Breadth ft-ins	Depth in hold ft-ins	Burthen tons
Design	105-0	86-1¼	28-6	13-10	372
As completed					
Hecla	105-0	86-1	29-0	13-11	375
Infernal	105-0	86-1	28-4	13-10	374
Fury	102		27		326
Meteor	106-0	87-1	28-11	13-10	
Ætna	105-2	86-1	28-1	13-10	375
Sulphur	105-4	86-2	28-11	13-10	375
Erebus	105-0	86-1	28-10	13-10	372
Thunder	108-6	105-1?	28-8	20-0	471

Building data

Name	Ordered	Builder	Laid down	Launched	Fate
Hecla	1813	Barkworth & Hawkes, Hull	Jul 1813	22 Jul 1815	Sold 1831
Infernal	1813	Barkworth & Hawkes, Hull	Jul 1813	26 Jul 1815	Sold 1831
Fury	1813?	Mrs Ross, Rochester	Sep 1813	4 Apr 1814	Lost 1825
Meteor	1819?	Pembroke Dyd	May 1820	25 Jun 1823	Sold 1846
Ætna	1819?	Chatham Dyd	Sep 1821	14 May 1824	Hulked 1839
Sulphur	1819?	Chatham Dyd	May 1824	26 Jan 1826	Hulked 1843
Erebus	1823?	Pembroke Dyd	Oct 1824	7 Jun 1826	Lost 1848
Thunder	1819?	Deptford Dyd	Nov 1826	4 Aug 1829	BU 1851

reorganisation of naval administration in 1831-32. The struggle for improvement continued to the last, the Surveyors being asked to report on the state of the bomb beds of ships after the battle of Algiers, with a view to suggesting improvements in this new class.[100]

They can claim to be the last purpose-built bombs in the Royal Navy, although naturally most of them found other peacetime duties, either as exploration vessels – *Hecla*, *Fury* and *Erebus* – or as survey vessels in the case of *Meteor*, *Ætna*, *Sulphur* and *Thunder*. This preserved a pool of vessels which could be called on if required for active service, while giving them a useful role in the meantime. That there was still a strategic requirement for these vessels has been made quite clear by recent research, which stresses the importance of coastal attack in British war planning.[101]

However by the outbreak of the next conflict in the Crimea and Baltic none of the *Vesuvius* or *Hecla* class vessels was still in service. What then

Table 41: *MORTAR VESSEL NUMBER 2*, 1854
Specification

Armament:	Mortars	Secondary		Men
Design				
As completed	1x10in			

	Gun deck ft-ins	Keel ft-ins	Breadth ft-ins	Depth in hold ft-ins	Burthen tons
Design					
As completed					
Mortar Vessel Number 2	60-1	47-6	20-9	9-0	105

Notes: Mortar Vessel Number 2 was built as a dock lighter named *Sinbad*, converted to a bomb in 1854, reverted to her original use in 1856 and finally broken up in 1866.

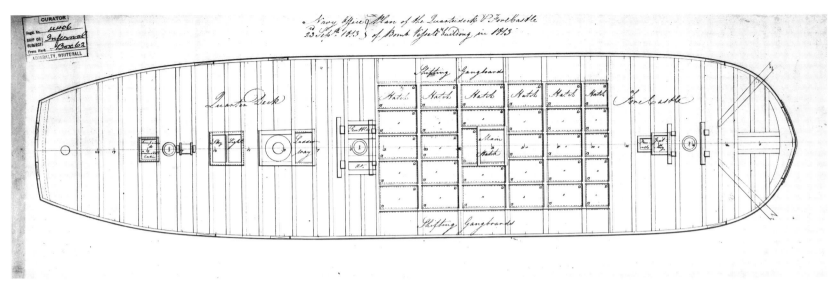

Infernal, 1815, design quarterdeck and forecastle plan.

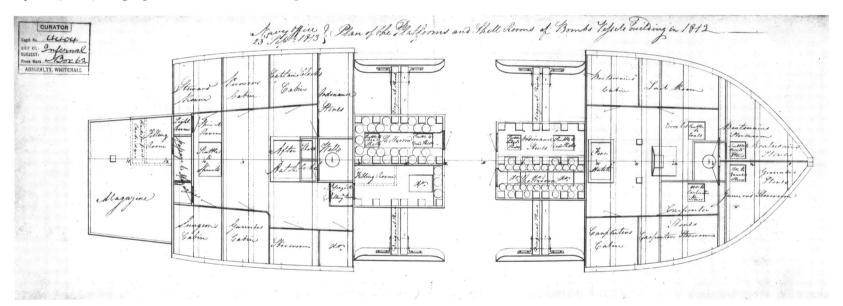

Infernal, 1815, design platforms and shell rooms plan.

happened was a repeat of the standard eighteenth-century response to the shortage, *ie* resorting to rapid conversion. The *Sinbad*, a dockyard sailing lighter, was adapted in 1854 at the height of the war to carry a single mortar.

Sinbad was renamed *Mortar Vessel Number 2* when converted, and although in no sense a seagoing bomb she is a convenient conclusion to the story of the shore bombardment vessel in the Age of Sail. Mortars were also fitted into converted screw frigates and these may be regarded as the immediate descendants of the sailing bomb; longer term, the First World War monitor was an exact equivalent, and appropriately two of the most characteristic bomb names, *Erebus* and *Terror*, were re-employed for one class.

The one question that recurs throughout the story of the bomb is whether they were cost-effective. Under the pressure of war much use was made of improvisation and modification, so was the purpose-built bomb really necessary to a navy whose resources were always scarce? Properly designed vessels were undoubtedly better, but to what degree is almost impossible to decide. They were primarily only carriers of mortars, so the more ship-like characteristics were secondary – and it might well be argued that the more sloop-like hull forms of the mid eighteenth century achieved some speed only at the expense of their qualities as stable gun platforms, and the final designs opted for more capacious hulls. However, purpose-building did allow the working out of the best systems for mounting and operating mortars: as Jackie Fisher said later 'The Royal Navy always travels first class', so perhaps it was inevitable that such a navy would demand the best.

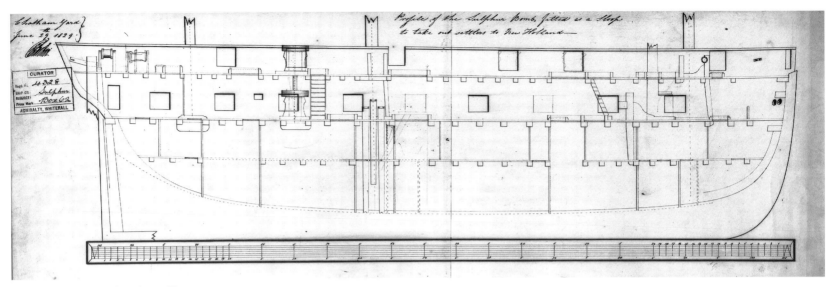

Sulphur, 1826, as fitted profile.

This drawing shows the *Sulphur* when she was fitted as a sloop to carry settlers out to New Holland. The mortar beds and their supports have been removed and two continuous decks put in their place. The longevity of the design is evidenced by the building date, some thirteen years after the first vessel of the class.

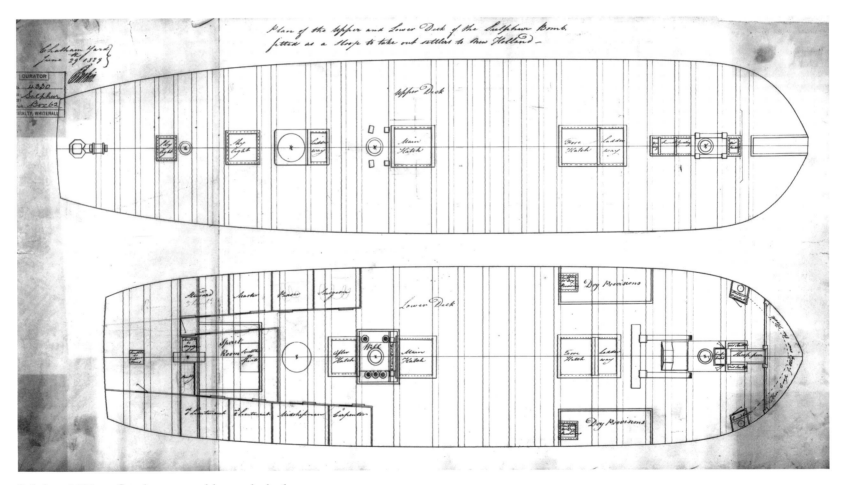

Sulphur, 1826, as fitted upper and lower deck plans.

This plan show the two decks fitted for her voyage to take settlers out to New Holland in 1829.

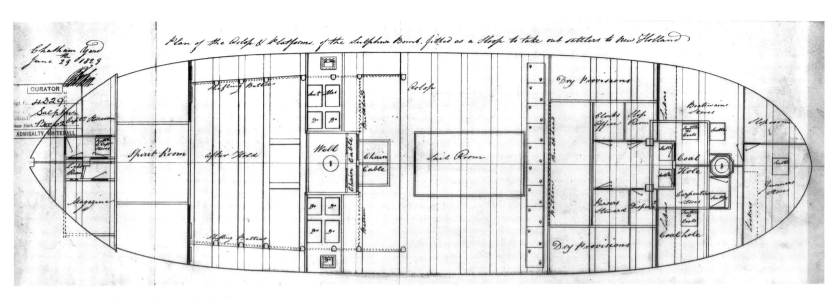

Sulphur, 1826, as fitted orlop and platforms plan.

The sail room and carpenter's store room had to be moved when she was fitted as a sloop. In this plan the sail room is almost amidships instead of on the port side forward under the forecastle.

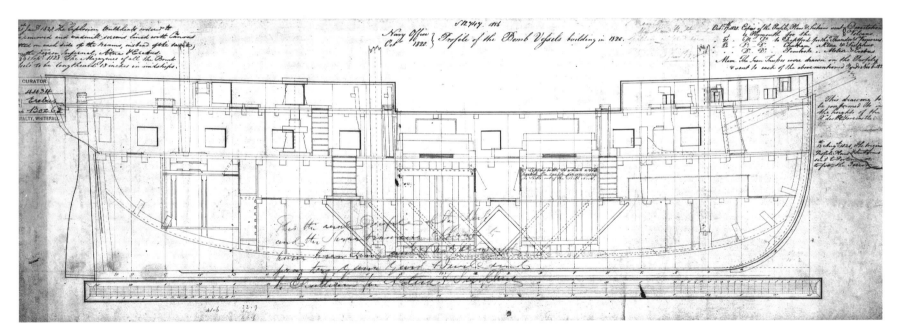

Erebus, 1826, design inboard profile.

As well as showing the usual features of the *Hecla* class of bomb, this view of the *Erebus* shows the diagonal iron bracing which was coming into use at about this time. It is not shown on any of the other inboard profiles for this class.

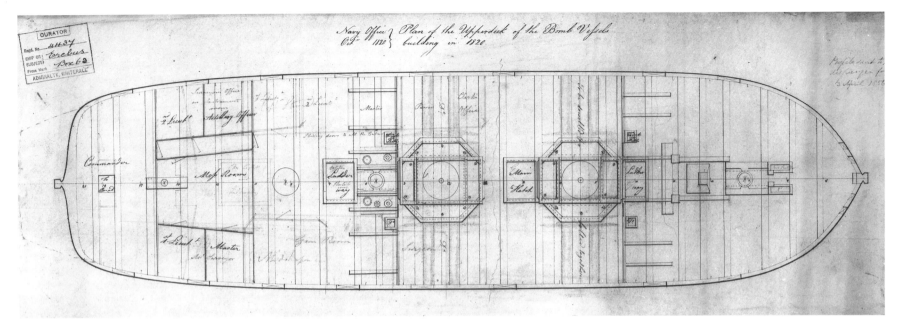

Erebus, 1826, design upper deck plan.

Just visible on this plan are the alterations made when she was converted to Arctic service.

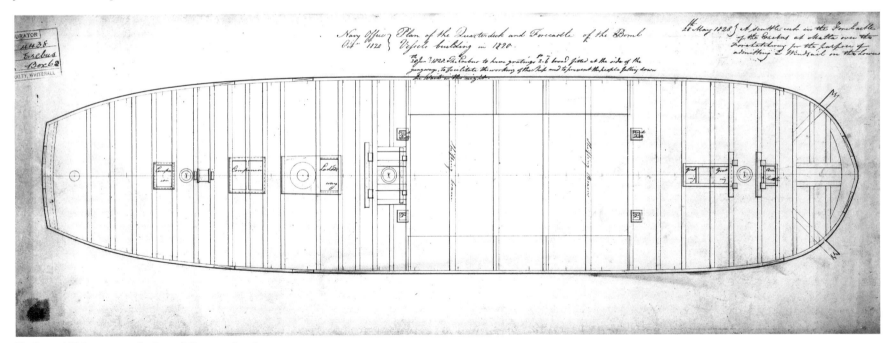

Erebus, 1826, quarterdeck and forecastle plan.

Quarterdeck and forecastle as built as a bomb vessel.

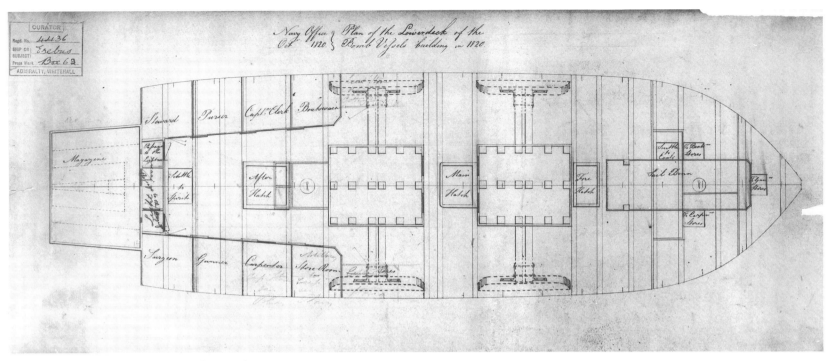

Erebus, 1826, lower deck and platforms plan.

This plan is as built as a bomb with the standard layout of cabins and store rooms.

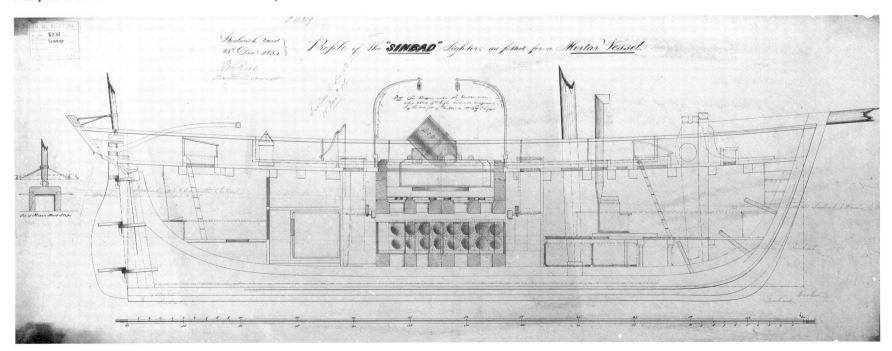

Sinbad, 1854, as fitted inboard profile.

The *Sinbad* was a conversion and in many ways with her the bomb came almost full circle. Single mortar in a small hull.

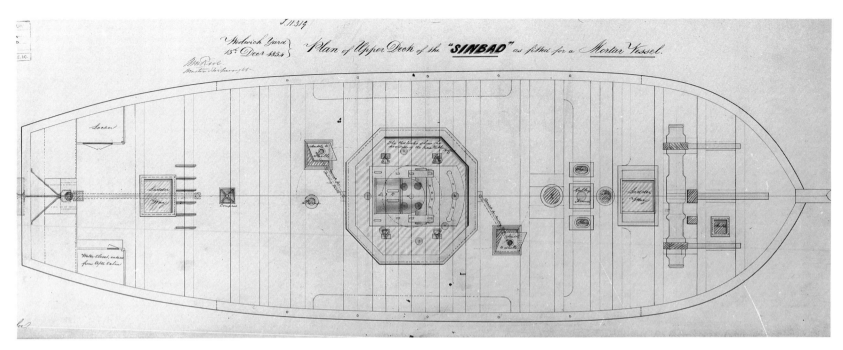

Sinbad, 1854, as fitted upper deck plan.

The single mortar dominates the space on the upper deck. What is also noticeable is that she carries a windlass, not a capstan, which would have been a disadvantage if she had to use springs in action.

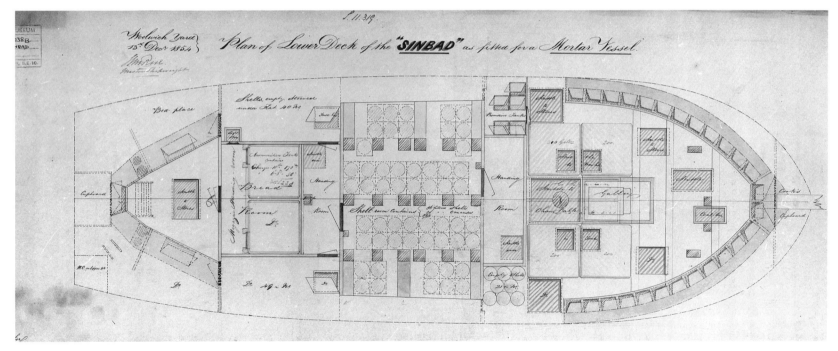

Sinbad, 1854, as fitted lower deck plan.

The cramped below decks are clearly shown here. Every spare space is used to stow empty shells.

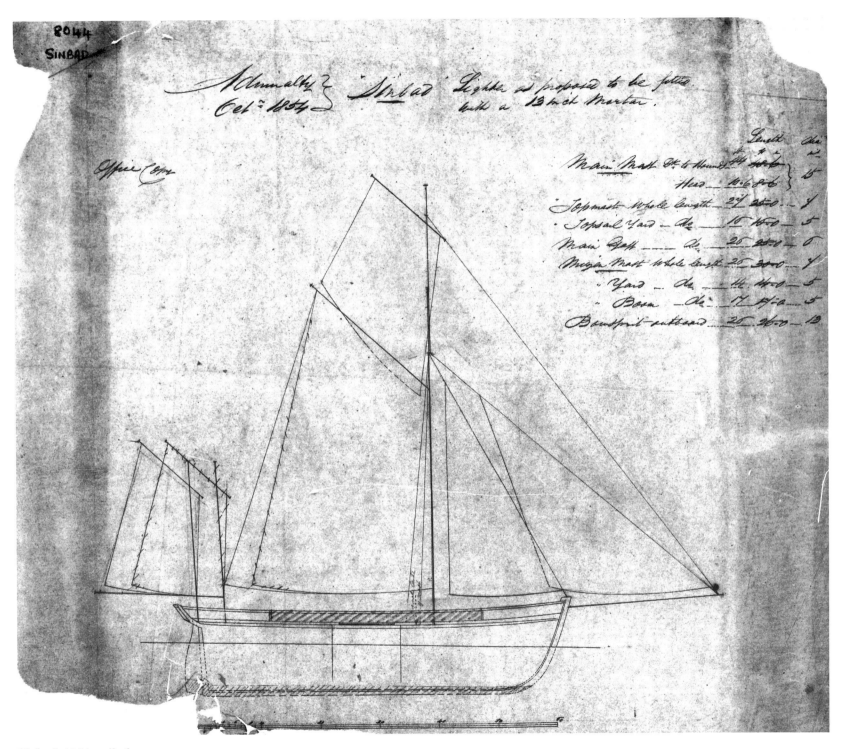

Sinbad, 1854, sail plan.

In this she looks more like a nineteenth-century coasting ketch than the last of the sailing bomb vessels. The rig would not have greatly interfered with the working of the mortar.

Meteor, ex-*Star,* section of mortar bed and shell room, 1811.

The sloop *Star* was altered during construction; like the later ex-mercantile vessels,
she had diagonal bracing in the hold to support the weight of the mortar beds.

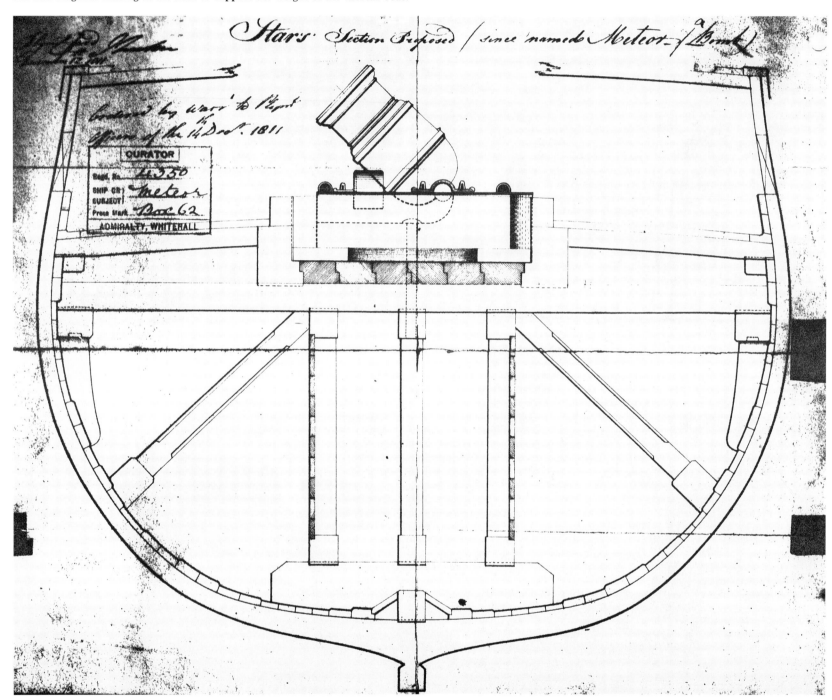

Part 2: The Ships

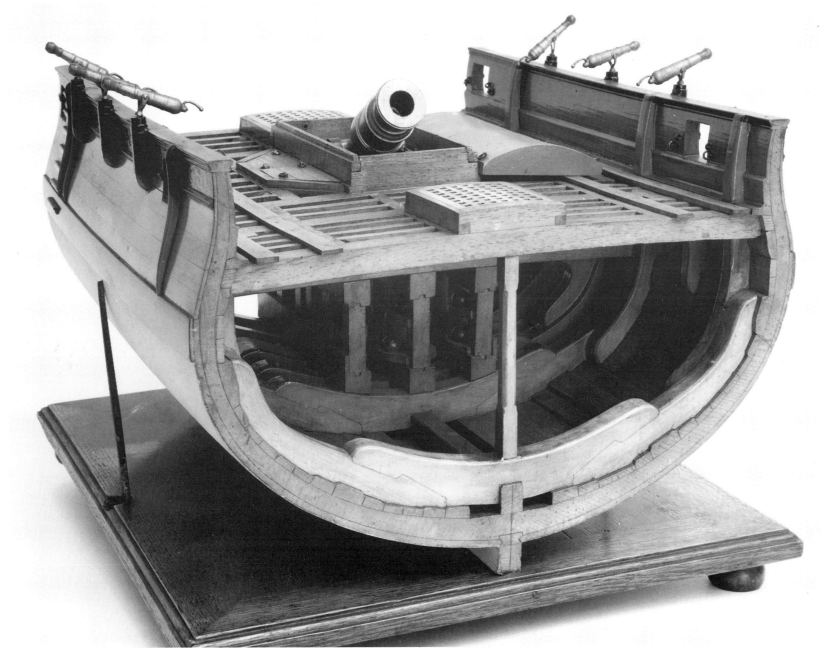

Contemporary eighteenth-century model bomb vessel, midships section.

This model is one of the few contemporary models of bomb vessels, showing to good effect the hull form and supports for the mortar beds.

8. The Structure of the Bomb

THE LAYOUT AND INTERNAL ARRANGEMENTS of the bomb vessel were unlike any other small or, come to that, large vessel of the age of sail, being entirely designed around the mortars and their infrastructure. Some idea was given of the nature of the mortar pits and their supports in the previous chapter when discussing the *Perseus*. As well as the eighteen pillars and beams, running fore and aft they had carlings the whole length of the 'beds 16 up and down in broad, placed 9ft 2in asunder.'[102] One specialist fitting was the bomb room, which in the case of the *Perseus* was 'to be 8ft square, 10ft in the beam, enclosed with thick coamings caulked and made tight as high as the deck.'[103] Around the pillars the specification called for 'plank round the outside of the outer tier of pillars from the bomb beds the edge to be rebated, and lined on the inside with slit deal, with a plaiting of lime and hair on the inside.'[104] To facilitate the stowage and transfer of the shells there were 'proper moving platforms fixed in rows of elm plank 4in and as broad as the distance between pillars will admit, with circular beds cut out in them agreeable in diameter to receive the shells.'[105] A 13in shell weighed 200lbs, so it is not surprising that moving platforms were necessary, and these may be regarded as a small step down the road to the mechanised

Sketch of a bomb room in a mid eighteenth-century vessel.

The fitting of the bomb room as portrayed in a model at the National Maritime Museum. *(Drawn by David Wray)*

A modern model of the *Granado*, 1742.

Starboard side view of R A Lightley's model showing the frame spacing and between-decks detail. The bomb rooms are clearly visible in this view. In front of the model are the sweeps (long oars), the ports for which are spaced between the gun ports on the upper deck

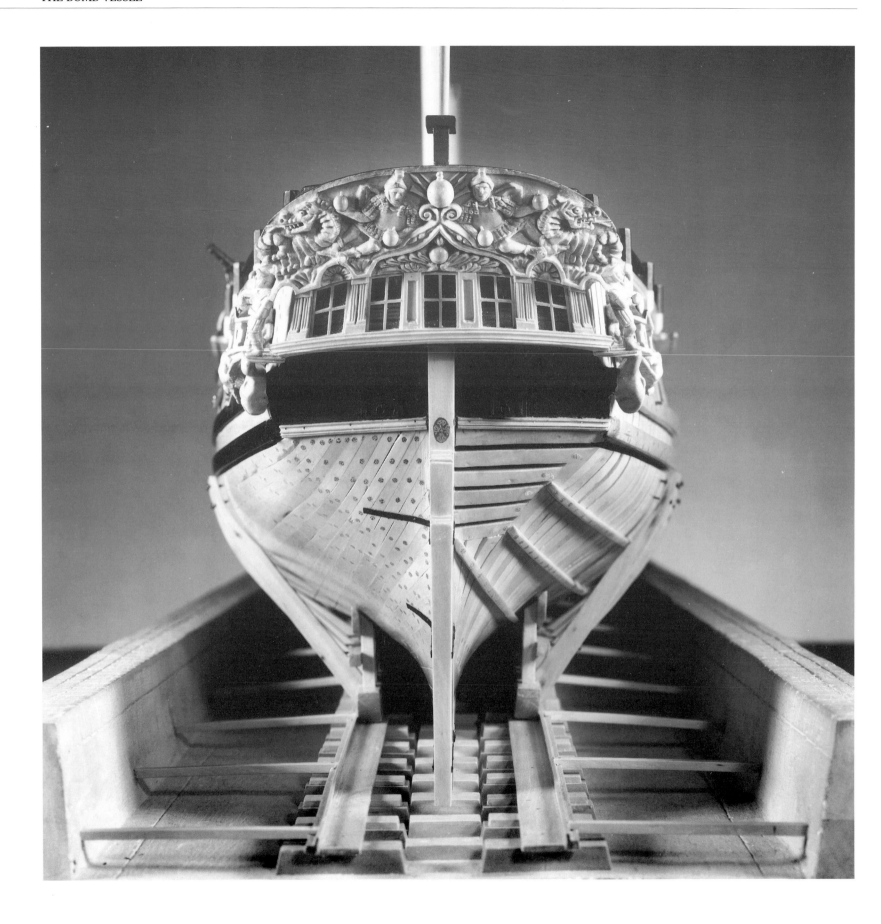

and automated magazines of twentieth-century warships. Another point of interest is the fact that the interior of the bomb room was plastered with the same fireproof mixture which was used to render houses of the same period!

Above the pillars and bomb room were the mortar pits themselves.

In the earliest bombs, and indeed until the 1740s, the pits and mortars had no fixed covering. Initially this was probably because the mortars themselves were cast in one piece with their bed and at a fixed elevation. As such the equivalent of a small deckhouse would have been required to cover them, and in any case the mortars were often removed to the

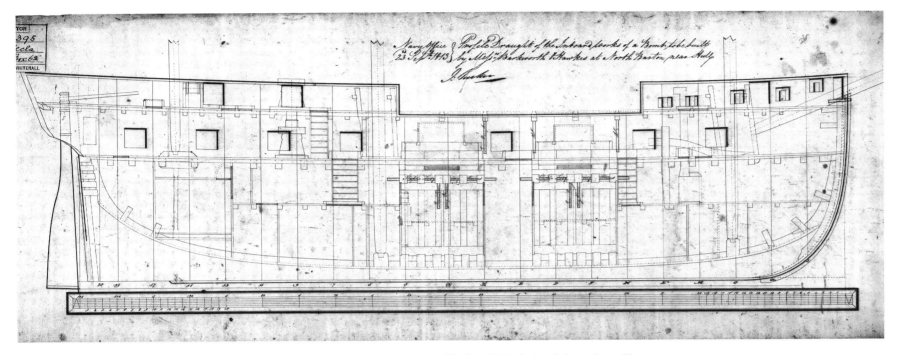

A modern model of the *Granado*, 1742.

Stern view of the model of the *Granado*. This vessel was unusual in not having the narrow pink stern: indeed the full-width stern was decorated with elaborate carvings which were not usually lavished on vessels which were not expected to last long in service. The bas-relief figures on the taffrail give a clear indication of the *Granado*'s purpose, holding as they do grenades (often called 'granadoes' at this time) in both hands.

Hecla, 1813, design inboard profile.

Draughts of the later classes often give plenty of detail of the internal layout and structure of bomb vessels. The bomb beds and hatch coverings are clearly depicted in this profile drawing.

Hecla, 1813, design upper deck plan.

The *Hecla* class followed the same deck layout as the *Vesuvius* class.

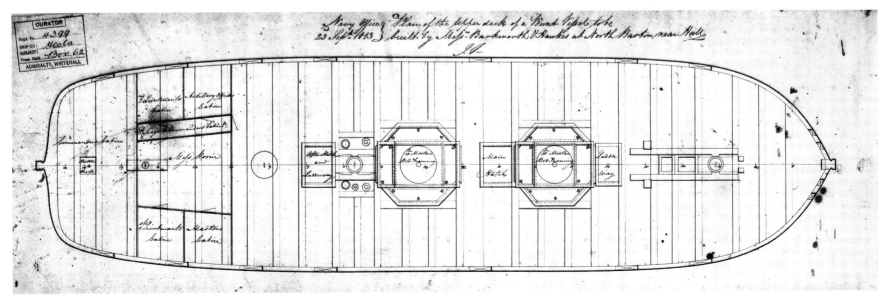

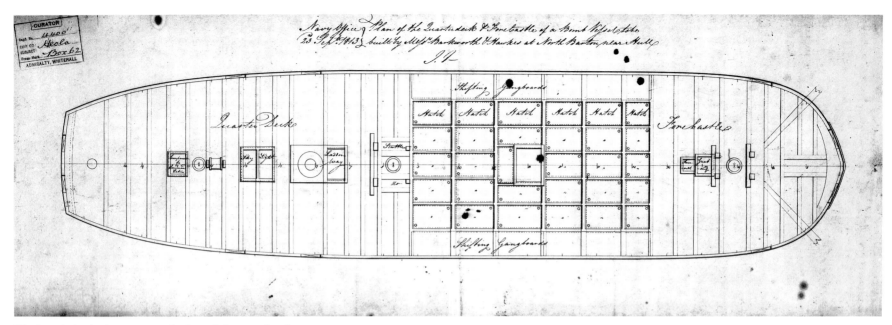

Hecla, 1813, design quarterdeck and forecastle plan.

This class were fitted with 'shifting' (removable) gangboards and full hatch coverings, allowing the mortars an unprecedented degree of protection.

Block model of the *Erebus*.

Two views: This contemporary model shows the hull form of the last of the large sailing bomb vessels to good effect. They still retain the bluff bow and the near flat bottoms of previous types.

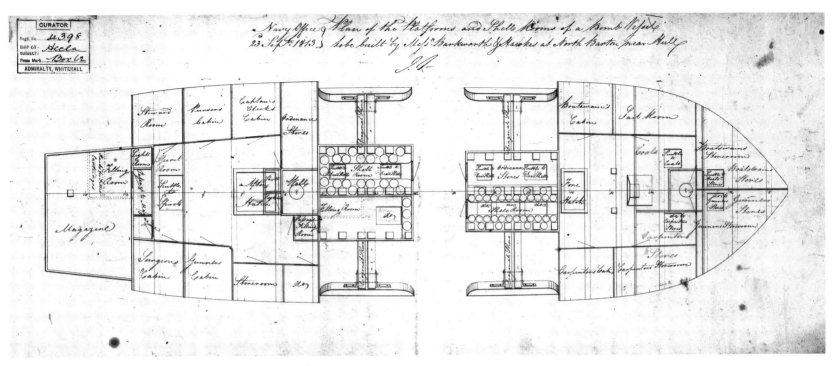

Hecla class, 1813, design platform and shell rooms plan.

The *Hecla* class were the ultimate in the sailing bomb vessel. As mentioned in the text they carried a greater provision of shells and carcasses than previous vessels. The two shell rooms are clearly visible but what is of interest is the magazine right aft with the filling room sandwiching the warrant and petty officers cabin between the two spaces. This clearly illustrates that even this late on crew space was at a premium.

Table 42: MAST AND SPAR DIMENSIONS

Salamander (based on Keltridge, 1683)

	Mast in Yards	Yards in Yards
Main mast	23½	15
Topmast	10	9
Topgallant	4⅓	4⅓
Mizzen mast	14	14
Topmast	5⅓	4⅓
Crojack		9
Bowsprit	13	
Spritsail yard		9

Terror and Comet 1742

	Mast (yds)	Diam (ins)	Spars (yds)	Diam (ins)
Main mast	24	24	18²⁴/₃₆	13
Topmast	14	12½	13¹²/₃₆	8
Topgallant	7	7	7¹²/₃₆	4¾
Mizzen mast	20	16		
Topmast	8²⁴/₃₆	7½	7²⁶/₃₆	4¾
Topgallant	4¹²/₃₆	4¼	7²⁰/₃₆	3
Bowsprit	16²⁰/₃₆	20		
Crossjack			13¹²/₃₆	8
Gaff			6	4
Wing gaff			6	5

Carcass 1757

	Mast (yds-ins)	Diam (ins)	Spars (yds-ins)	Diam (ins)
Main mast	22-0	19½	18-6	12½
Topmast	13-7	11⅞	13-10	8⅝
Topgallant	6-28	6⅝	8-6	4⅞
Fore mast	19-24	17⅛	16	11⅛
Topmast	11-24	11⅞	11-24	7¼
Topgallant	5-23	5¾	7-6	4½
Mizzen to step	15-12	12¼	8-6	7
Mizzen on deck*	18-2			
Topmast	9-24	7¾	8-25	5¾
Bowsprit	13-14	18⅞	11-24	7¼
Jibboom	10-0	9	8-6	4⅞
Crossjack			11-24	7¼

*The length of the mast to the step in the hold must be greater than when stepped on deck, so perhaps this should read 12yds 2ins, the clerk having added instead of subtracting.

tender when on passage. The only other alternative would have been to dismount them as the French did and lay them on their sides in the pits, but there is no evidence that such was the British practice. By 1728 mortars were cast with trunnions which allowed them to be adjusted for elevation, and when not in use laid horizontal (see the following chapter). The coaming which had always be a part of the structure of the pit was raised and covers provided to keep the mortars and their mounting dry.

Because of the placement of the mortar beds and the pillars to support them, the bomb vessels of the eighteenth century did not have a continuous deck below the upper deck. There were platform decks fore and aft which served in the stern for commissioned and warrant officer accommodation and bread room, etc; forward, from keel up, there was the cable tier, and galley, with the crew squeezed in the remaining space. Reference has already been made to the need to remove the pillars and other reinforcements when operating in their secondary role as sloops. This was because a larger crew was established in the cruising role, since the bomb then carried more guns, and there would have been insufficient room for berthing the crew and stowing provisions. The fact that the firing crew were accommodated aboard the bomb tender had everything to do with lack of space below decks.

RIG

The rig of the bomb vessel for almost the first seventy years of its service was the ketch, although there had been an early experiment with ship rigged vessels in the *Mortar* class, but this was not followed up. There were logical reasons for the ketch rig, in that it allowed the minimum obstruction to the mortars, with one forward of and the other sited in between the main mast and mizzen. In the earliest vessels with one mortar only, or a pair abreast, this rig would have allowed the ship's principal weapon to be sited forward of any substantial obstruction, *eg* a mast. The introduction of the trainable mounting allowed a fore and aft centreline arrangement of mortars which in theory might have reduced the need for bomb vessels to be ketch rigged, but in practice it merely allowed the main mast to be stepped further forward, giving a better balanced sail plan. Sloops, with which bomb vessels had much in common including size, were given two-masted rigs until the 1750s, so it should not be surprising that the ship rig was not again assayed for bombs until the *Infernal*s of the same period.

However, the ketch rig also suffered some distinct disadvantages in that the area of canvas was very unevenly divided between main and mizzen, and often the position of the main was dictated by the mortar beds rather than the requirements of a balanced rig. Furthermore, in order to give these ketches a satisfactory total sail area, the main was often proportionately very tall. The aggregate result were the kind of problems highlighted by the sailing reports quoted in earlier chapters: over-masting, carrying lee helm, exaggerated rolling, poor windward performance, and sluggish sailing.

Table 42 gives the spar dimensions for a selection of bombs, including the ship rigged *Carcass*. Length of mast and yards is given in

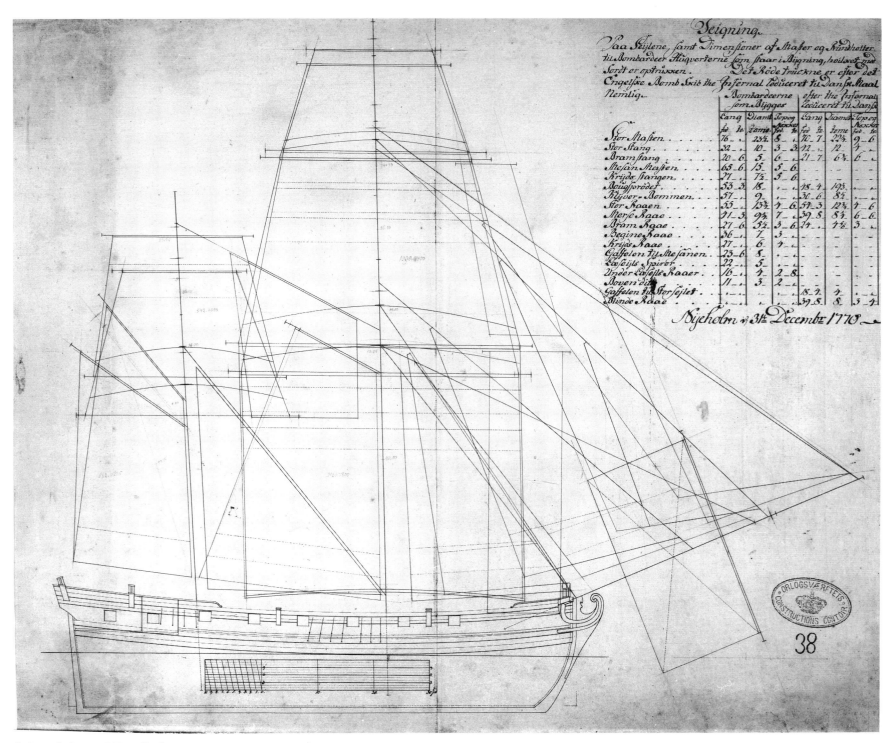

Infernal class, 1757, sail plan.

Sail plans are almost unknown in the eighteenth-century Admiralty Collection, but there are a few in other sources, like this Danish draught. It shows the original sail plan of the 1757 ketches, with the cut-down sizes proposed in 1773 for a class of Danish bombs (with a rig known in Danish as *hukkert* or 'hooker'). The main gaff, or wingsail, is a notable feature of the rig. *(Rigsarkivet, Copenhagen)*

yards and fractions of yards, the diameter of spars in inches. A feature of ketch rigged bombs was a large gaff-headed fore-and-aft sail carried on the main; it was known as the wingsail, and the dimensions of its gaff are given below.

As noted previously, there are a number of recorded occasions when captains of bombs complained of their commands being over-masted and the dimensions for the *Comet* would seem to give support to this, with a main mast which from keel to truck was 135ft and a mizzen just under 99ft. This combination of the lofty proportions of the sail plan and the hull form goes some way to explaining the relatively poor handling characteristics of the ketch rigged bomb vessels in particular. On the other hand, in ship rigged bombs the problem of over-masting

was less commented on, but the setting up of the rig was still relatively sensitive. On the whole the ship rigged bomb vessels appear to have preformed fairly well, although there are still occasional references to three-masted bombs missing stays when tacking in anything but calm seas. As sailing vessels the bombs were not the swiftest or the handiest, but this is not surprising given the compromises necessary in the design of the type, whatever the rig.

Bombardment of Fort Royal, Guadaloupe, 1745

The bomb vessels in this view are not well executed, but their position behind the major warships is quite plausible. These vessels would have been of the *Basilisk* class.

9. *The Bomb Vessel in Action*

THE BOMB VESSEL WAS A floating siege engine, and as such the way in which it accomplished its task was radically different from that of other warships. The requirement was for deliberate, aimed fire (as against rapid, short range broadsides), and a consequence of this was the need to know the exact range to the target, and to fire from a steady platform.

The bomb vessel in action should also be sheltered, whenever possible, from the attentions of the defences, so as not to expose the ship or to allow counter-battery fire to upset the aim of the artillerymen. Aboard the vessel itself during the bombardment there was need for strict regimentation. The quantity of shells and powder actually carried aboard may have been limited but, when in action the charge for the mortar and the gunpowder filling of shells needed careful regulations for their handling if serious consequences for the vessel itself were not to ensue.

Sea service mortar.

This mortar is cast with its base and could only change range by either adjusting the powder change or moving the vessel. When not in action these mortars were often shipped aboard larger vessels. *(The Tower Armouries)*

The number of shells and carcasses which could be carried aboard a bomb vessel was limited by the space below deck and the size and weight of the projectiles themselves. A 13in shell was a little over twice the diameter and six times the weight of a 32pdr solid shot. In the 1690s the provision for shell and carcasses aboard a bomb vessel was set at '60 rounds of bombs and 10 rounds of carcasses for each mortar'.[107] This was to be supplemented aboard the transports with '440 rounds of bombs and 40 of carcasses on board the tenders'.[108] This same provision of 120 rounds of shells and 20 carcass to be carried aboard each bomb vessel was still the norm in the War of Spanish Succession, but there is evidence that the last bomb designs of 1812-13 were intended to carry a larger allowance. The amount of additional ammunition carried aboard the bomb tender was in the ratio of 44 shells to every one round of carcass. These were to be split equally between the two mortars.

THE COST

The cost of fitting out a bomb vessel with mortars and ordnance stores in the 1690s is examined in Table 43.

Table 43: COSTS OF A BOMB VESSEL, 1690s[109]

Total charge for fitting out a bomb vessel

A mortar of 13in and all materials and officers to attended	£3479-5s-1¼d
The mortar @ 120s a ton	£60-0
For two carriages for the same	£140-0
Bombs of 12¾in 500 in number – weight 50 tons @ £14-0 per ton	£700-0
125 carcasses @ £14-0	£175-0
750 Fuses @ 4½d	£14-1-3d
Vessel of 100 tons as a tender	£480-0

Table 43 includes most of the major stores and also the price of the bomb tender as well as the pay of the officers of the Ordnance who would fire the mortars. The total cost for the supply of ordnance when compared to the price estimated for building the 1695 group of bombs given in Chapter 1 – which came out at £2056-0 for the hull, masts and rigging – means that the price to get a bomb vessel fitted out and supplied with ordnance stores was some £1423 more than the cost of the hull and fittings alone. Thus the aggregate cost for one bomb vessel, from the laying of the keel to being fitting out with her mortars, would have been £5535-05s. This would be minus the wages of the officers and seamen who manned the vessel. In the same document as quoted above, the price of ordnance stores for ten bombs equipped with twenty mortars was estimated at £99,460-12s-8½d, this total including the wages of the officers and men to attend the mortars. This was the number of bomb vessels sent out in 1695-96 and gives an idea of the pressure such operations put on the resources of the nation. If to this is added the price of the hulls for the bomb vessels built during the year, the total expended for 1695 on bomb vessels was £117,964-12s. In general shipbuilding terms, this could have provided for the construction of another 5-6 Third Rates.

A decade later in 1705 the estimates for supply ordnance stores for nine bombs to fitted for that year amounted to £26,428-5s-7d. The cost of fitting out with ordnance stores thirty-two Third Rates of 70 guns during the same period totalled £21,253-10s-0¾d. Therefore even after the initial expense of building and equipping a bomb vessel had been incurred there would have been a significant annual expenditure to keep them in service each year they were employed as bomb vessels.

ORDNANCE DEVELOPMENT

The one signal difference which has been highlighted between French and British bomb vessels was the rapid strides made by the latter in the fitting of the mortars. The French remained with fixed mortars firing over the bow of the vessel, but the British were quick to develop something more flexible. The earliest English classes were probably similar to equivalent French vessels in layout, but the spur to a major change appears to have come from the aftermath of the bombardment of St Malo in 1693.[110]

On 23 February 1694 five men were appointed to look into the question of 'fixing mortars so as they should be more serviceable'. Those appointed were Colonels Richards and Bourne of the Board of Ordnance, Captains Leake and Silver of the Navy and the émigré Frenchman, Fournier, who was retained by the navy to advise on the construction of bomb vessels. The same day as their appointment all five gentlemen went to Deptford to examine the bomb vessels there. On the next day, 24 February, several proposals were put up to the Board of Ordnance (unfortunately none of the alternatives is mentioned in the minutes), and 'that by Colonel Richards was approved and a letter to Colonel Richards was written (who had undertooke to contrive a way to make the mortars traversable on board the vessels) to take sole management of this affair upon himself.'

The first vessels to be fitted with Richards' traversable mounting would be the *Firedrake*, *Granado*, *Salamander*, *Portsmouth*, and *Kitchen*. These alterations were to be undertaken by Mr Hardy, the master builder at Deptford, and occurred right at the very end of February. The decision to mount mortars on turntables went through with great expedition, less than three weeks having elapsed between investigation and implementation.

Colonel Richards was a fervent believer in the value of the mortar, although less practical in his understanding of the shortcomings of the ship as a gun platform. In December 1694 he proposed building a great galleass, to be armed with 24 5-ton mortars (12 on each broadside); the theoretical advantages of a craft that could be rowed into position were obvious in the bombardment role, but the naval architectural ramifications were beyond his comprehension. The Navy Board, busy with more practical problems, was forced to calculate that such a ship would be about 1550 tons, as wide as, and 10ft longer than, an 80-gun ship, costing £19,760.[111] Visionary as this might seem, it was not entirely an original inspiration, since earlier in the year the British consul at Genoa had forwarded a proposal by a Venetian shipwright to build a galleass for the Royal Navy; once again the Navy Board had to point out with

Model of an eighteenth-century bronze mortar.

Probably a sea service 13in of the pattern that became common from the 1730s onwards. *(The Tower Armouries)*

as much patience as it could muster why such a craft was unsuitable for British needs.

The remainder of Colonel Richards' tasks for 1694 were more mundane, but fraught with trouble. As touched on earlier, the twelve vessels he was to hire proved more difficult to obtain than at first anticipated. There were also problems with the supply of the mortars themselves, which were only ordered as the vessels that were to carry them were being hired. As a consequence, when the contractors for the mortars could not deliver them on time, there were delays in getting the bombs to sea, which in turn led to the investigation upon which

proceedings this account is based.

Once the new principle was accepted, the practical side of fitting out all of the bomb vessels with the new mounting had to be addressed. In February 1695 the Admiralty ordered twelve bombs to be fitted out, but the Ordnance 'acquainted them that the carriages for mortars to traverse upon are the most serviceable which is our opinion... yet considering with how much more expedition the mortars may be placed in fix'd carriages, propose to fix 6 new mortars in 6 several vessels by reason they cannot be traversed and the 6 old ones in three others in their old traversable carriages'.[112] Thus despite the advantages which would ensue from the fitting of mortars on the new mounting, the exigences of the service meant that it was quicker to fit the old and have a mixed force of traversable and non-traversable mountings.

The new mountings (which had become standard by the start of the War of the Spanish Succession in 1702) endowed the bomb vessel with

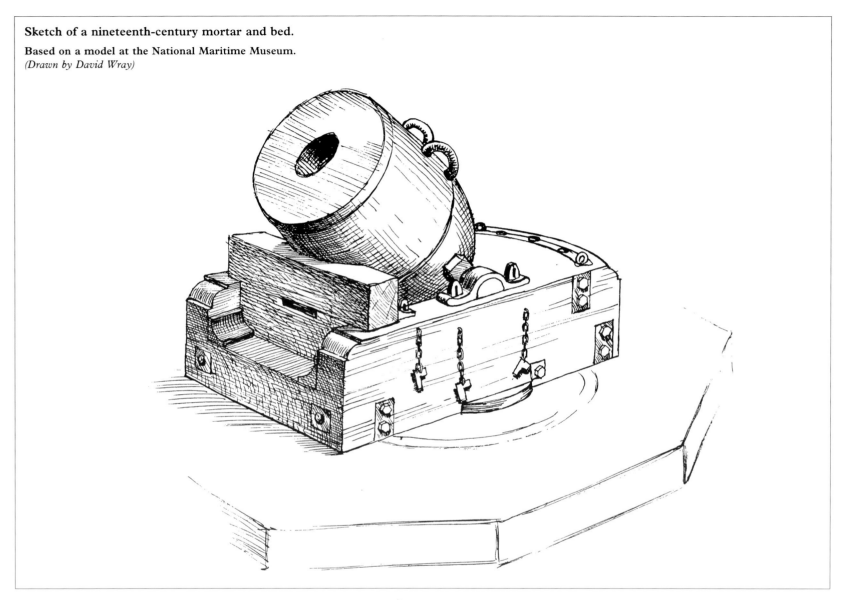

Sketch of a nineteenth-century mortar and bed.

Based on a model at the National Maritime Museum.
(Drawn by David Wray)

a great degree of freedom in their firing stations. There were still the practical difficulties of firing through rigging (which have already been alluded to), but the fact the they could lay broadside on to a target or at 60 degrees to it gave a greater flexibility to their commanders than had been possible previously.

The actual mounting was based on a wooden plinth with a metal pintle, or axle, which allowed the carriage to rotate. Movement was imparted to the turntable in earlier bomb vessels by a kind of ratchet device, but this soon fell out of favour and blocks, tackles and hand spikes seem to have been the norm for the greater part of the eighteenth century.

Until the 1720s the mortars were cast at a fixed elevation of 45 degrees, but the Tower Armouries have a bronze sea service 13in mortar with base-mounted trunnions known to have been cast in 1726.[113] This is the first recorded example, and since the Tower of London was an ordnance repository for much of its history, this weapon may be the prototype of the so-called 'Trabucco' type. This first went to sea with the new bomb vessels of 1728, so allowing for some experimentation the timing makes such an identification distinctly possible. The trunnions at the base allowed the mortar to be elevated to the required angle and a wooden (later iron) chock was used to keep it in place; previous to this, range could only be altered by varying the powder charge.

Table 44 gives the weight of the standard projectiles and the theoretical range of typical 10in and 13in mortars.

These are only examples, but they given an impression of the weight of fire and the theoretical range available from bomb vessels. The firing charge was between 10lbs and 15lbs of powder for a 13in mortar and 6lbs 4oz for a 10in weapon.

Development went on throughout the eighteenth century, although improvement was incremental rather than radical. The mortars were

Table 44: SEA SERVICE MORTARS

13in Sea Mortar

Type	Weight cwt-qtr-lb	Weight of shell in yards	Range at 45°
Brass	88-2-6	197lb plus 10lb 4oz bursting charge	4100

10in Sea Mortar

Type	Weight cwt-qtr-lb	Weight of shell in yards	Range at 45°
Iron	41	92lb plus 4lb bursting charge	4000

rarely able to sustain prolonged bombardment – although the same could be said for the vessels themselves, which always required a thorough refit after a major action. Nevertheless, attempts were made at improved casting and there were some developments in design. For example, Colonel Shrapnel, who gave his name to the fragmentation shell, invented a 10in brass mortar with a parabolic chamber that was the same size as the sea service iron 10in but had superior range. It was quickly approved by the Admiralty, but longer testing showed it to be dangerous and it was not issued.[114]

More successful was a new pattern introduced in 1812. At that time there were three sea service models: a 13in of 4 tons 2cwt, a 'long' 10in of 2 tons 8cwt, and a 'short' 10in of 2 tons 2cwt. These were replaced by new pattern weapons of 5 tons 0cwt (13in) and 2 tons 12cwt (10in), and were first fitted in the bombs of 1812.[115] *Hecla* and later bombs also introduced a chock moved by a ratchet system which made it easier to make alterations to the elevation.[116]

SUPPORTING THE BOMB VESSEL

A major element in getting the bomb vessel into action was the tender, which accompanied all bombs on active service. From the Board of Ordnance minutes it is quite clear that tenders were hired on the open market and then converted for their specialist employment; normally the tender was hired for just one season. The conversion consisted of having bulkheads fixed in the holds and suitable stowage for the bombs and carcasses. There were sometimes disputes with the masters/owners about how much work could be done to their vessels and when it could be undertaken. On the last point most owners would not allow their vessel to be altered until the financial aspects of the contract were settled.[117] The vessel themselves were approximately 100 tons and more often than not pinks. Table 45 lists those vessels hired for use as tenders in the campaign of 1695, the earliest listing of such vessels.

Throughout the eighteenth century the size of the tenders grew very little, so by the 1780s they were still less than 150 tons maximum – a ship rigged vessel of a little over 150 tons was turned down in the 1780s as too large for the task.

Aboard the tender was not just the reserve ammunition and powder

Table 45: HIRED TENDERS, 1695[118]

Mary	Pink	*Thomas and Elizabeth*	Hoy
Charity	Pink	*Brotherhood*	Pink
Seaflower	Pink	*Thomas and Christian*	Hoy
Grassthorp Park	Ketch	*Fristan*	Yacht
Happie Return	Pink	*Bonadventure*	Pink

but also the Ordnance personnel who manned the mortars in action. The commander of the detachment was entitled to one sixteen-oared boat, which appears to have been used to transfer shells, etc as well carrying the commander. This boat was supplemented when in action by boats drawn from the protecting fleet. No boats were carried on the bomb vessels themselves.

MANNING THE BOMB IN ACTION

There was a clear division from the earliest employment of bombs between the sea service who sailed the vessel itself and the men who actually fired the mortars, a divide that reached right up to the officers who commanded them. There was also a separate staff structure to control the Ordnance contingent when sent out as a major adjunct to the fleet, and this is outlined in Table 46. The same command structure appears to hold good for both of William's wars (the War of the League of Augsburg and the War of the Spanish Succession).

From this it is clear that the Ordnance did not see themselves as subordinate to the sea officers when afloat. They had a complete structure which looked after the needs (both spiritual and temporal) of Ordnance personnel whilst afloat, and enabled them to operate autonomously from the Navy. As well as the officers who commanded the contingent, there were aboard the tenders the bombardiers who fired the mortars and the fireworker who superintended the filling and fusing of the shells. The bombardiers were assisted both in firing and transferring the shells and carcasses by a detachment of the ship's company.

The responsibility for firing the mortars was taken over in 1804 by the newly-established Royal Marine Artillery. This made much of the support for bomb vessels an Admiralty concern, although the mortars, like all naval guns, were still supplied by the Board of Ordnance. The new arrangement obviously took some time to establish itself in the mind of the Admiralty, for as late as 1807 it was instructing the Ordnance to provide tenders for *Zebra*, *Fury*, *Vesuvius* and *Thunder*, only to be told that it was now Their Lordships' responsibility.[120]

Table 46: ORDNANCE STAFF FOR BOMB VESSELS[119]

Colonel	Firemaster	5 other smiths
Lieut-Colonel	Surgeon	Master tinman
Major	Surgeon's mate	His assistant
Paymaster	Master carpenter	Commissary
Chaplain	Master smith	

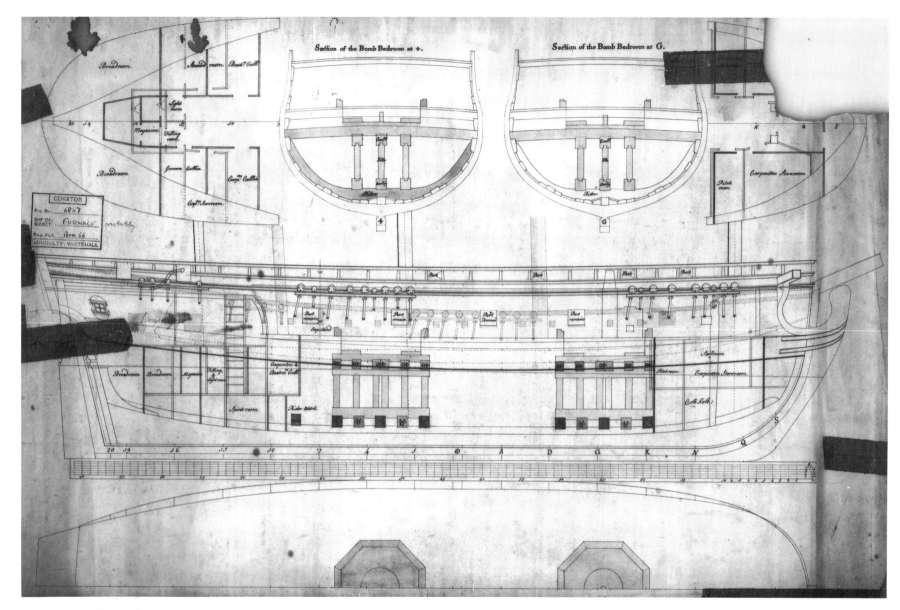

Furnace, profile, platforms and sections of proposed conversion to Arctic exploration vessel, 1740.

This appears to to be a first attempt at a conversion without the removal of the bomb beds and shell rooms.

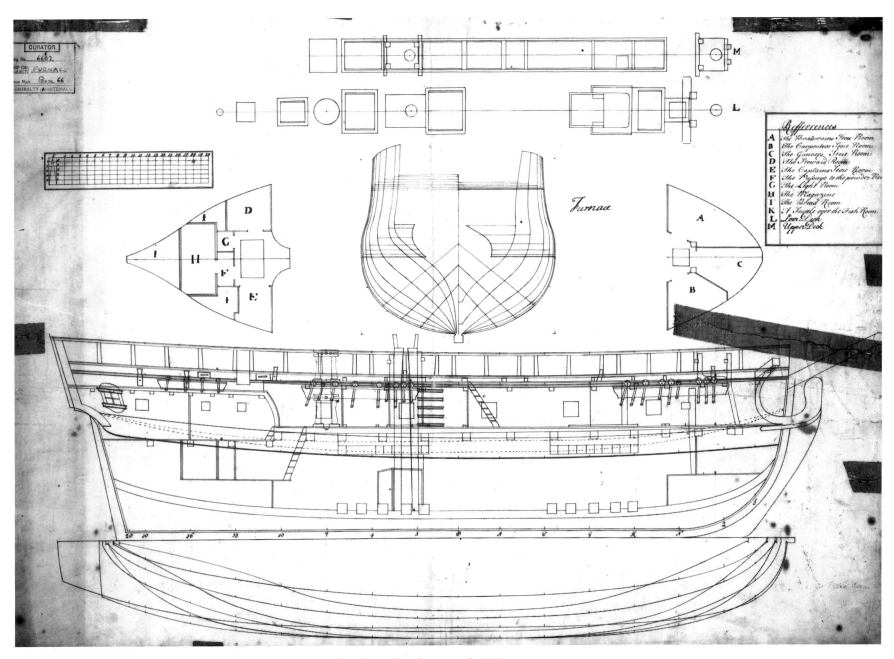

Furnace, profile, platforms and sections as converted to Arctic exploration vessel, 1740.

Compared with the sheer plan opposite, this version of the draught shows a number of modifications in the below-decks arrangements – most noticably the removal of the mortar beds and shell rooms – but also incorporates some of the features specifically requested by Captain Middleton, including the full naval double capstan.

10. Poles Apart

THE EXTENSIVE USE OF BOMB vessels for exploration in the eighteenth and nineteenth centuries is not surprising. The flowering of scientific – as against purely territorially acquisitive – voyages in the eighteenth century found the Royal Navy providing both ships and men for such expeditions. The bomb vessel was peculiarly well suited to Arctic voyages. The squarish midship section, bluff bow and strong construction of the hull (to withstand the firing of the mortars) meant that the bomb vessel had the right combination of strength and internal capacity – if the mortar beds were removed – to withstand the rigours of the weather peculiar to that region, and in particular the ice conditions. Table 47 lists the bomb vessel used for Arctic exploration.

Although the bomb vessel possessed many advantages, what it did not have – at least in the earliest vessels – was a continuous lower deck. There was also the fact that (as has been discussed earlier) bombs were by and large not good sea-boats and many lacked freeboard. These disadvantages were brought home in a letter from Captain Middleton to the Navy Board dated 21 March 1740 concerning the fitting out of the *Furnace* for an Arctic voyage: 'Having proposed the raising of her sides about two feet fore and aft and to lay another deck on her, in order to make her more wholesome in the sea, and convenient for storing Men and Provisions, keep the men as dry as possible and preserve their

Table 47: BOMBS CONVERTED FOR POLAR EXPLORATION

Name	When built	Arctic exploration
Furnace	1740	1741
Carcass	1759	1773-5
Racehorse	1757	1773-5
Fury	1814	1821
Terror	1813	1836 and 1845
Erebus	1826	1839 and 1845

health.'[121] The letter goes on to discuss the fitting of a capstan in place of the windlass, as it would be necessary to anchor in deep water.

The Admiralty ordered that the work be carried out as follows:

Raise the gunwale of the said sloop fore and aft two feet and six inches and a fife rail fore and aft of about one foot three inches above that of sufficient height to secure the men and to lay a light deck from the fore part of the quarterdeck to the stern, to be five feet six inches between plank and plank.

They also ordered that the windlass be removed, to be replaced with a capstan, and a fireplace and double kettle be fitted between decks. The

Carcass, 1773, profile and section as fitted for Arctic service.

The reinforcing of the bows is shown in these plans, as is the fact that the bomb beds have been landed, although some of the pillars are still there.

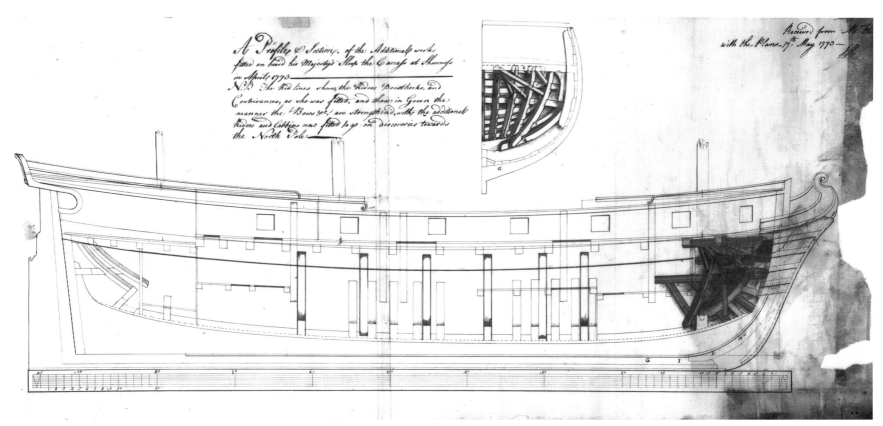

Racehorse and *Carcass* in the ice, 1773.

The view of the two vessels in the ice shows the boats which were carried for the voyages to the Arctic. It would appear that most of the crew are on the ice hauling the ships' boats, on the stern of one of which is the ship's fiddler, playing as the men work.

oar ports below the gun ports were to be sealed and alternatives placed on the upper deck, along with the pumps. The arrangement of the cabin was also altered at the same time. Four officers would have to berth in the steerage, namely the Lieutenant, Boatswain, Carpenter and Master's Mate. What is plain from both the letter and the draughts is that the *Furnace* underwent considerable alteration to get her ready for service. The fact that the bomb was designed to be dual purpose may have assisted in as much as the bomb beds were relatively easy to remove (and, perhaps more importantly, to replace).

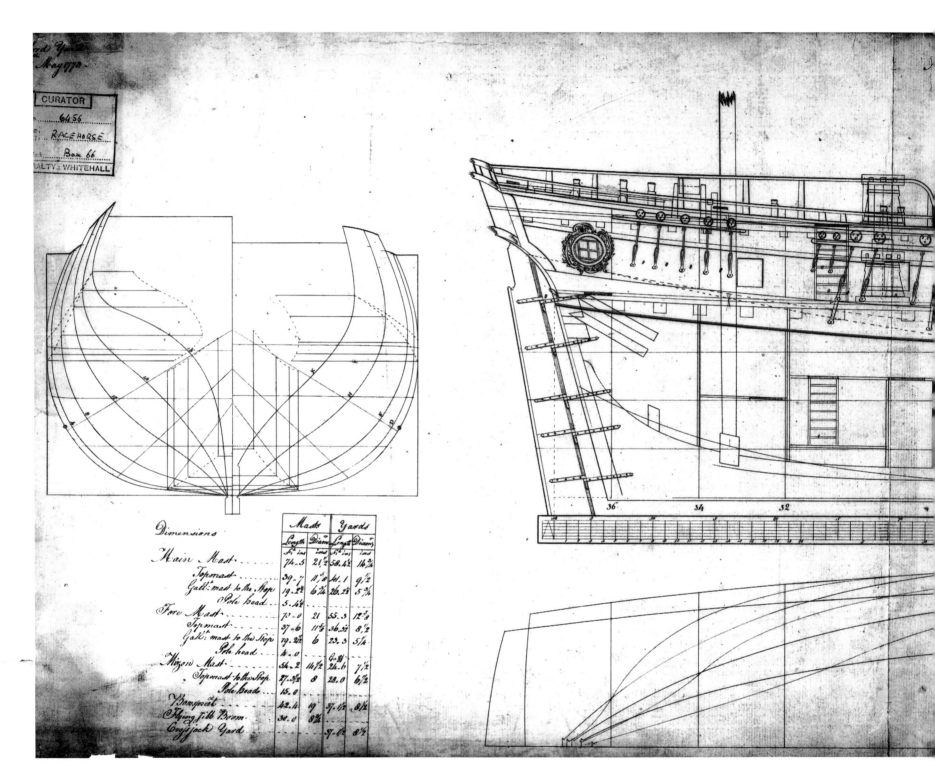

Racehorse, 1773, inboard profile and lines as fitted for Arctic service.

Racehorse was fitted with a double deck to accommodate the extra crew and stores for the voyage north.

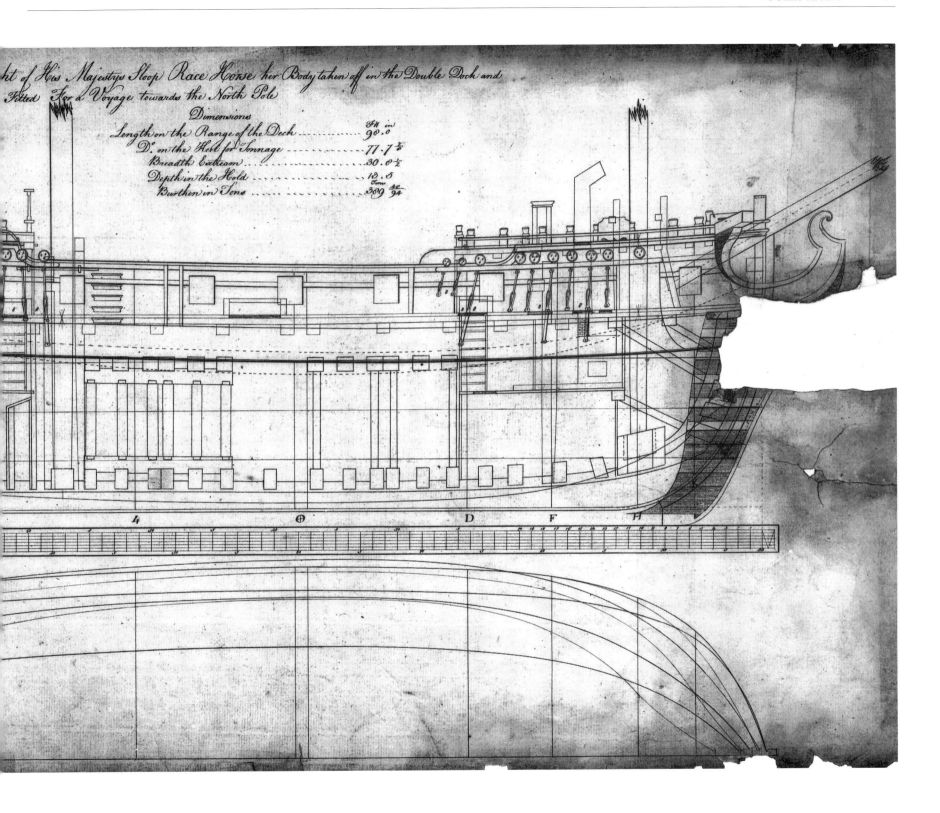

...ht of His Majestys Sloop Race Horse her Body taken off in the Double Dock and Fitted for a Voyage towards the North Pole

Dimensions

		Ft in
Length on the Range of the Deck		90.0
Do. on the Keel for Tonnage		77.7½
Breadth Extream		30.8½
Depth in the Hold		13.5
Burthen in Tons		389 40/94

Carcass, 1773, as fitted upper, quarter, forecastle and orlop plans.

This was not strictly a refit for the Arctic but when she was used to go to the Falklands in the 1760s as an exploration vessel.

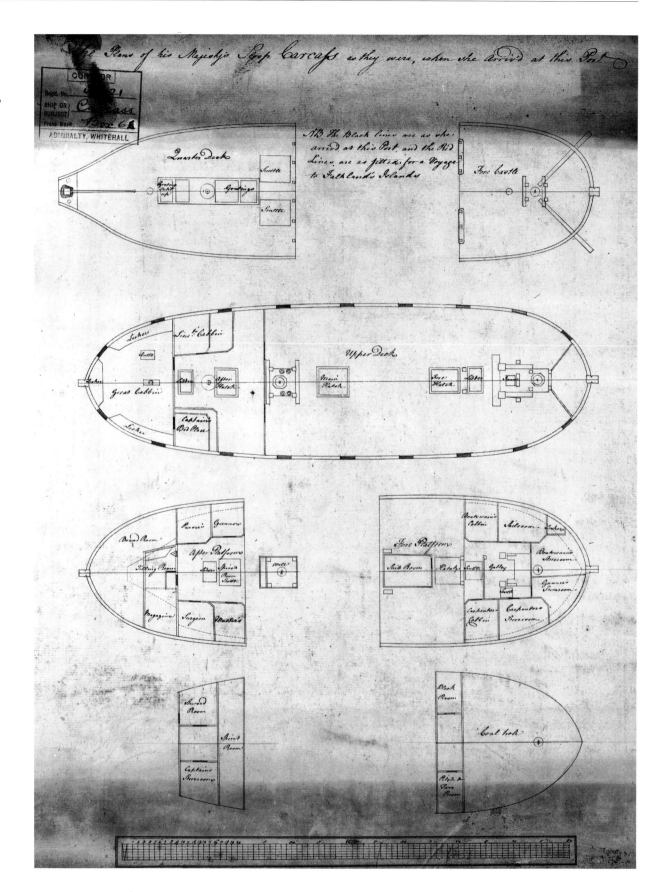

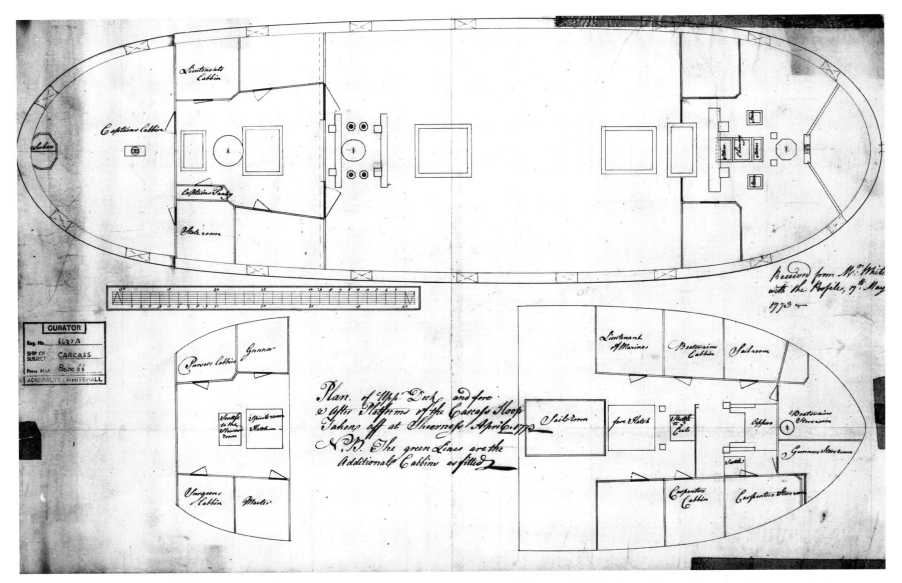

Carcass, 1773, as fitted deck and platforms plans.

These plans show the additional cabins need for her Arctic service. As was the case with all such alterations, they were marked in green on the original.

What is not mentioned in the case of the *Furnace* but was to become a feature with other bombs going into the ice was the reinforcing of the bows, as when the *Racehorse* and *Carcass* went to the Arctic in 1773. This voyage, to be commanded by Phipps, required two bomb vessels to be fitted out for the task. The Navy Board proposed the following measures be taken to fit them for the Arctic: 'that the bottoms of said sloops may be doubled; their bows fortified by breasthooks and sleepers, and additional riders added in the space between the bomb bed.'[122] As well as the structural alterations to the hulls, the two ships were provided with a double set of ice poles, anchors and cables, plus two suits of sails. The two vessels were also to be equipped with boats (something they did not carry when serving as bombs) which were to be of sufficient capacity to carry all of the crew if either vessel were lost. As a last resort both *Racehorse* and *Carcass* were provided with bricks and mortar to build a shelter if both were cast away on shore.

The crew were also to be specially fitted out for Arctic service. They were to be issued with two flannel jackets, cotton shirts, cotton handkerchiefs, two lined fearnought jackets, two lined waistcoats, two milled yarn caps, one pair of boots, two pairs of boot stockings, two pairs of fearnought trousers and twelve pairs of mittens. Thus the officers and crew seem to have undergone as much refurbishment as the ships themselves. The *Racehorse* also carried an apparatus for distilling fresh water from salt, which provide a great success, being able to provide between 30 and 40 gallons of water per day.

The last bomb vessel used in the Arctic underwent similar strengthening to bow, etc as is evident from the plans. They also had extra heating for the crew spaces. *Erebus* and *Terror* both went to the Arctic twice, once in 1836 and for the second time in 1845. For this latter

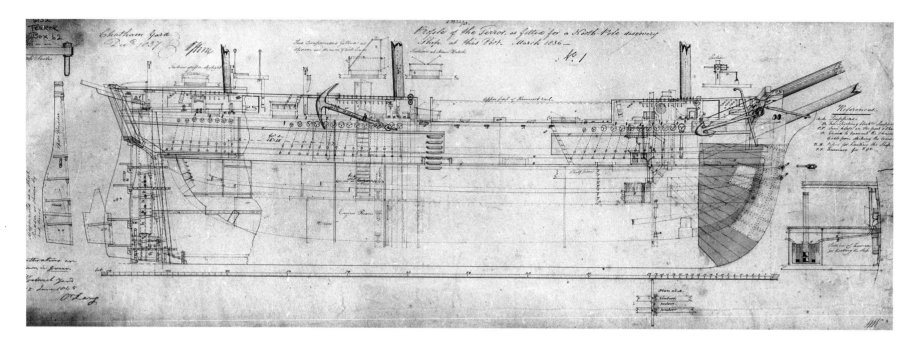

voyage the most radical modification was the adoption of auxiliary steam propulsion. This entailed cutting through the stern post, to allow the propeller shaft to be run through, and the fitting of a telescopic funnel to service the boiler. A hoisting screw, and detachable rudder were also fitted at the same time. The fact that neither of these vessel survived the 1845 Franklin voyage to the Arctic had nothing to do with the quality of the conversion they underwent and everthing to do with the provisions they carried. In fact it was not so much the provisions as the soldering on the cans, which it is now believed induced lead poisoning in the crews of both vessel. The tin can had been introduced

Terror, 1836, as fitted profile.

The reinforcing to the bows is shown on this plan as is the new heating system in the half section in the bottom right-hand corner.

Erebus and Terror, 1836, upper deck plan as fitted for Arctic service.

The stowage for the boats amidships and on the port and starboard quarters is visible on this plan. Also show is the flying bridge for navigation.

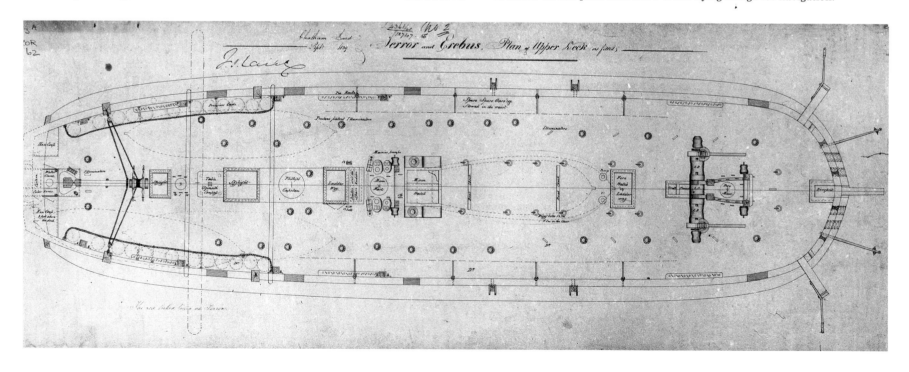

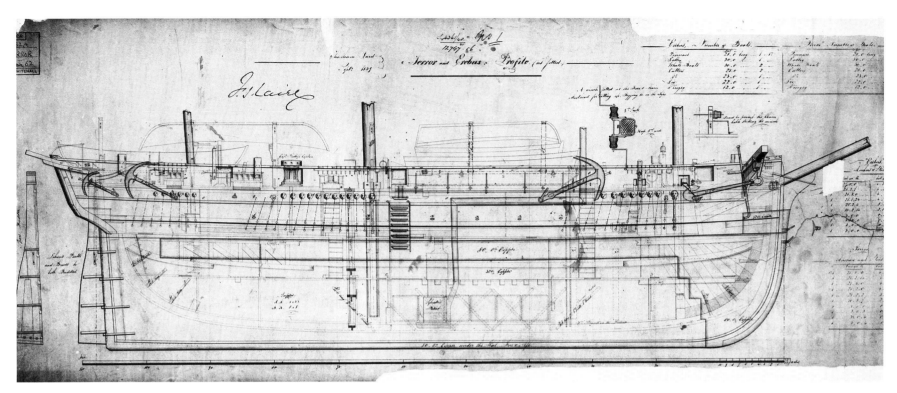

into naval service only some twenty years prior to the fateful voyage of the *Erebus* and *Terror* and its dangers were not fully understood.

This brief survey of the kinds of changes undertaken to fit the bomb for exploration work shows that the Admiralty literally built on the vessel's strengths. With the necessary modifications, bomb vessels survived to see their last service in this polar role, a role for which they were perhaps better suited than their usual peacetime employment as sloops.

Erebus and *Terror*, 1836, as fitted inboard profile.

This shows in greater detail the internal fittings as well as the boat stowage, compare this with the *Infernal* profile on page 67. There is no trace of their original role except the hull form.

Terror, 1836, as fitted plan of the upper deck.

Showing the increased size of the channel and the flying bridge as fitted for Arctic service.

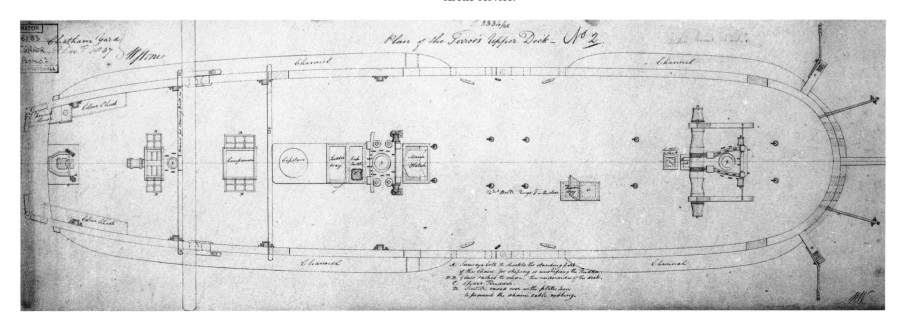

Erebus and *Terror*, 1836, as fitted midships section.

This view illustrates the extra sheathing which was applied to the outside of the hulls of these vessels to resist the ice.

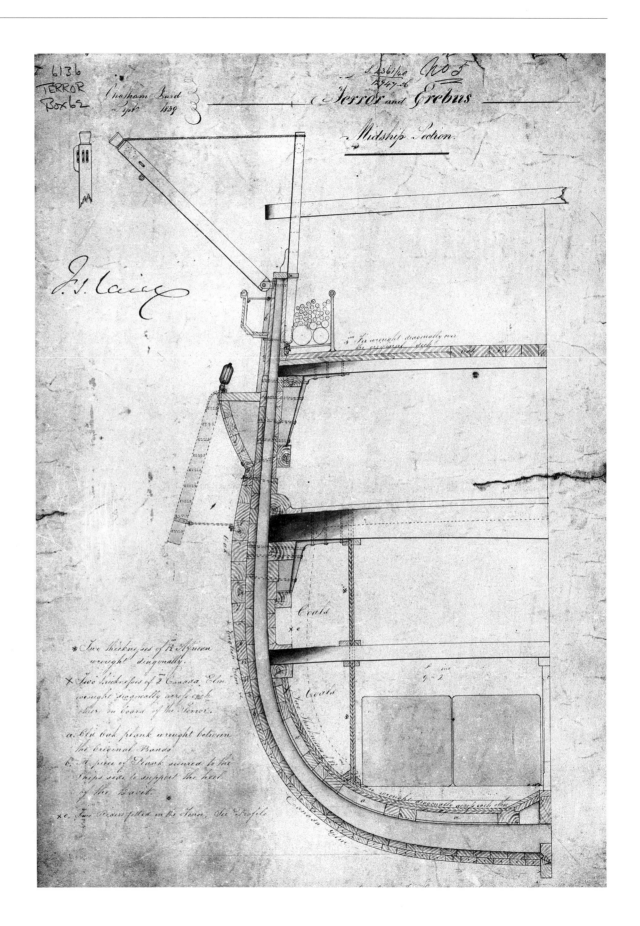

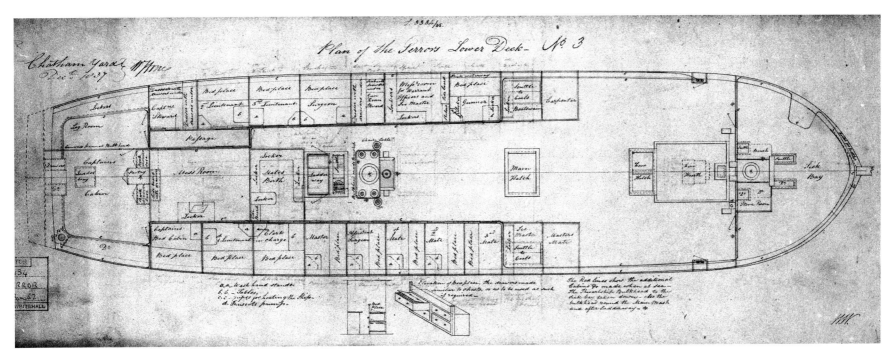

Terror, 1836, as fitted plan of the lower deck.

The greatly increased complement on these voyages meant that cabins took up two-thirds of the lower deck.

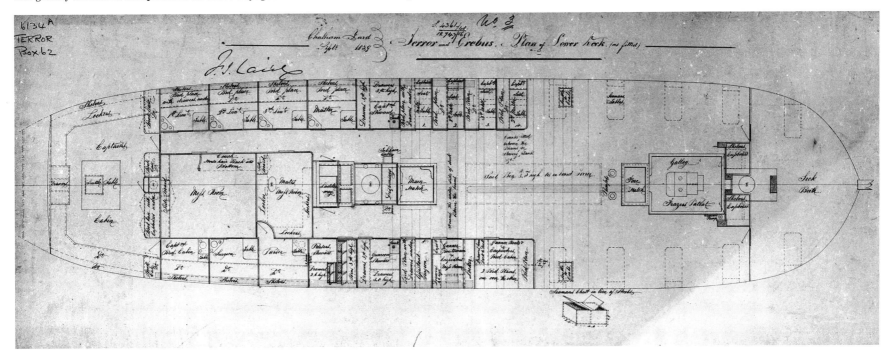

Erebus and *Terror*, 1836, as fitted plan of the lower deck.

This shows the lower deck in its final form.

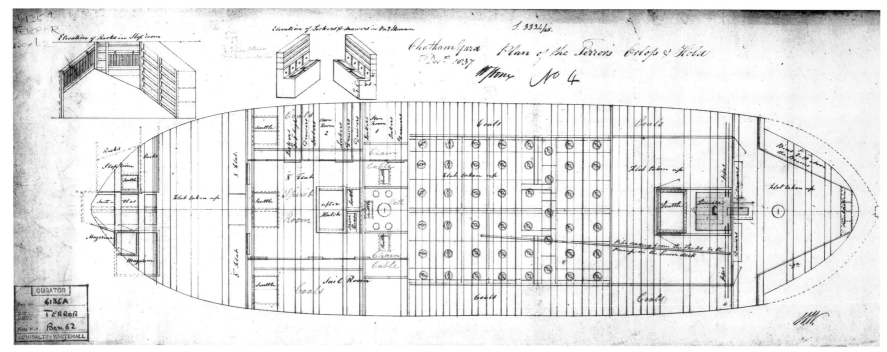

Terror, 1836, plan of the orlop deck.

This show the orlop when *Terror* was first fitted for the Arctic.

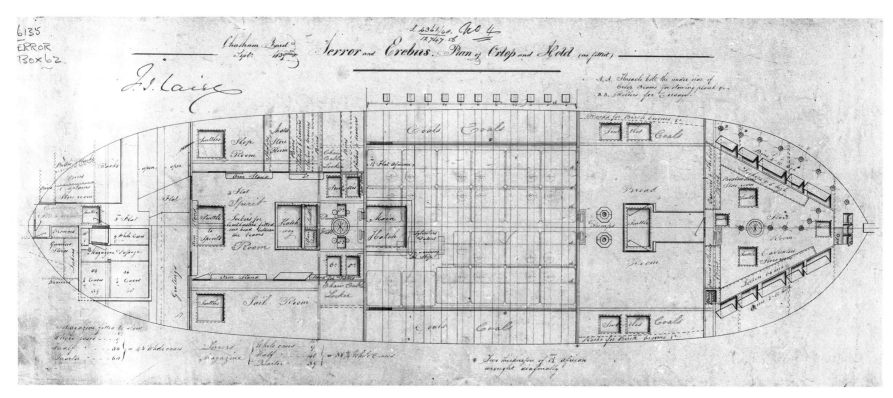

Erebus and *Terror*, 1836, plan of the orlop deck.

This is an as fitted plan for the two vessels.

Notes

[1] See Julian Corbett, *England in the Mediterranean 1600-1800* (London 1905), and also Gebb, *Piracy and the English Government 1601-1643* (Aldershot 1993).

[2] For a description of the genesis of the French bomb see J Boudriot and H Berti (trans D H Roberts), *The Bomb Ketch Salamandre* (Robertsbridge 1991), pp8-9.

[3] Boudriot, *Salamandre*, p20.

[4] Table 1 is drawn from information in Boudriot, *Salamandre*.

[5] Quoted by David Wray, 'Bomb vessels: their development and use, Part 1 1682-1700', *Model Shipwright* 19 (1977), p248.

[6] *Ibid*.

[7] D J Lyon, in *The Sailing Navy List* (London 1994), Chapter 2.

[8] Table based on D J Lyon, *The Sailing Navy List*. I am most grateful to David Lyon for sharing early versions of his work with me.

[9] PRO Adm 1/3556, letter of Nov 1687; and letter from Board of Ordnance 8 Jun 1688, both quoted in Wray, *op cit*, pp250-251. In the latter the mortars are specifically described as wrought iron for *Firedrake* and *Portsmouth*.

[10] Sergison, Navy Board to Admiralty, 21 August 1691; quoted in Wray, *op cit*, p250.

[11] Chapter 2 of D J Lyon, *The Sailing Navy List*.

[12] NMM CHA/L/6, letter of 27 Aug 1693.

[13] PRO Adm 1/3569, 14 Jun 1693.

[14] C R Markham, *The Life of Captain Stephen Martin*, Navy Records Society (London 1895), p46.

[15] PRO Adm 1/91 letter dated 28 January 1693.

[16] PRO Adm 1/91 letter dated 2 March 1692/3.

[17] PRO Adm 1/91 letter dated 22 March 1692/3.

[18] *Portsmouth* and *Firedrake* carried two 12¼in mortars (letter from the Board of Ordnance, 8 Jun 1688); and the four 1693 ships were allocated eight 13in weapons (royal warrant to Master General of the Ordnance, 11 Sep 1693): both quoted in Wray, *loc cit*, 19 (1977), p251 and 26 (1978), p20.

[19] *Ibid*, p47; he also shipped 16 guns.

[20] PRO Adm 1/3569, 29 Jun & 13 Jul 1693.

[21] NMM CHA/L/6, 15 Jul 1693. This was all very well, but a navy perennially short of small cruisers in wartime was unlikely to agree; indeed, throughout the remaining history of the bomb, the type was to find employment as sloops when not required for bombardment, and on occasion for a multiplicity of other minor roles.

[22] Markham, *op cit*, p27.

[23] *Ibid*, pp32, 37-38.

[24] See PRO War Office record WO 55/1749 for examples of stores provided and where they were to be fitted.

[25] PRO Adm 95/3, estimates 1688-92.

[26] Navy Board estimates in Adm 7/169, 1694-95.

[27] PRO Adm 7/172, navy estimates 1777-82, March 1782.

[28] PRO Adm 7/169, estimates 1688-1730, estimate dated 13 Jun 1694.

[29] PRO Adm 7/169, estimates 1688-1730.

[30] Introduction to Peter Goodwin, *The Bomb Vessel Granado, 1742* (London 1989).

[31] PRO WO 46/3, Ordnance Board Minutes, f29.

[32] PRO WO 46/3, Ordnance Board Minutes, ff29-33.

[33] PRO WO 46/3, Ordnance Board Minutes 1695, ff29-33.

[34] PRO WO 46/3, Ordnance Board Minutes 1695, ff31.

[35] PRO WO 46/3, Ordnance Board Minutes 1694-5. In this case all the papers relate to the purchase of the bomb vessels.

[36] J Lediard, *John Duke of Marlbrough*, (London 1735), Vol I, pp60-150.

[37] See the opening chapters of J H Owen, *War at Sea under Queen Anne* (Oxford 1938) for the problems of cruiser warfare.

[38] Figures given in Appendix B of *War at Sea under Queen Anne*.

[39] Those involved were the *Basilisk, Star, Furnace, Comet* and *Carcass*; see *War at Sea under Queen Anne*, pp149-151.

[40] Quoted in *War at Sea under Queen Anne*, p150.

[41] *War at Sea under Queen Anne*, p150.

[42] *War at Sea under Queen Anne*, p188.

[43] See the chapters on the War of the Spanish Succession in Josiah Burchett, *History of the Transactions at Sea* (London 1720).

[44] *War at Sea under Queen Anne*, p150.

[45] C R Markham, *The Life of Admiral Robert Fairfax* (London 1885).

[46] Quoted in *War at Sea under Queen Anne*, p189.

[47] PRO WO 47/33, Board of Ordnance Minutes 1705-6.

[48] PRO WO 47/23, Board of Ordnance Minutes 1705-6.

[49] D A Baugh, *British Naval Administration in the Age of Walpole* (Princeton 1965), p241.

[50] PRO Adm 106/2171, 26 Feb 1742: 'number of men and guns aboard the bombs now building, 60 men as a bomb vessels 90 men as a sloop'.

[51] See Howard Blackmore, *The Armouries of the Tower of London*, Vol 1: Ordnance (London 1976), catalogue item 102.

[52] See Wray, *Model Shipwright* 26 (1978), pp20-21.

[53] PRO Adm 95/25, sailing quality reports.

[54] PRO Adm 95/25, reports of sailing qualities.

[55] PRO Adm 106/2180, letter dated 20 Dec 1740.

[56] PRO Adm 106/2180, letter dated 20 Dec.

[57] See Chapter 6 of *War at Sea under Queen Anne*; the abstract of the log refers to smooth water and problems with wind and weather for firing.

[58] PRO Adm 106/2179, letter dated 7 Sept.

[59] PRO Adm 106/2178, Navy Board to Admiralty.

[60] PRO Adm 106/2178, 24 Jul 1740.

[61] See D J Lyon, *The Sailing Navy List* (London 1994), the most recent source to list their armament as 8 carriage guns.

[62] PRO Adm 106/2178, a series of letters concerning the armament of these vessels.

[63] PRO Adm 106/2178, letter dated 8 Oct.

[64] PRO Adm 106/2171, letter dated 7 Nov 1741.

[65] PRO Adm 106/2171, letter dated 7 Nov 1741.

[66] PRO Adm 106/2179, letter dated 16 Jun 1742.

[67] PRO Adm 106/2179, letter dated 16 Jun 1742.

[68] PRO Adm 106/2180, letter dated 26 Dec 1743.

[69] PRO Adm 106/2180, letter dated 27 Mar 1744.

[70] PRO Adm 106/2180, letters dated 7 Apr, 16 May and 13 Jun 1744.

[71] The *Granado* is the one British bomb for which there is a detailed study available. See P Goodwin, *The Bomb Vessel Granado, 1742* (London 1989).

[72] PRO Adm 95/30, sailing quality reports.

[73] PRO Adm 106/2171, letter dated 28 Jul 1742.

[74] NMM ADM/B/160, 8 Nov 1758.

[75] PRO Adm 106/2191, letter dated 8 Jan 1759.

[76] PRO Adm 95/84, Navy Board estimates 1774-83.

[77] PRO Adm 95/84, Navy Board estimates 1773-83.

[78] PRO Adm 106/2191, letter dated 1 Jan 1759.

[79] PRO Adm 95/28, sailing quality report dated Dec 1762.

[80] PRO Adm 95/34, sailing quality report dated 24 Jun 1763.

[81] PRO Adm 106/2192, letter dated 9 Jul 1759.

[82] PRO Adm 106/2191, letter dated 26 Apr 1759.

[83] PRO Adm 106/2191, letter dated 26 Apr 1759.

[84] See David Syrett, *The Royal Navy in American Waters* (Aldershot 1990).

[85] PRO Adm 95/33, sailing quality report.

[86] PRO Adm 95/30, sailing quality report.

[87] The following table is based on the Progress Books, held at the National Maritime Museum, which are copies of the originals held at the PRO (Adm 180/ series).

[88] PRO Adm 95/39, sailing trial report dated 1 Nov 1801.

[89] PRO Adm 95/85, undated but must be 1797.

[90] PRO Adm 95/85, f109.

[91] PRO Adm 106/2247, 11 Mar 1808.

[92] PRO Adm 95/48.

[93] PRO Adm 95/84, ff269-74.

[94] PRO Adm1/4020, 12 Jul 1811.

[95] PRO Adm1/4020, 10 Aug 1812; Board of Ordnance's response.

[96] PRO Adm 106/2257: the order to prepare the draughts was dated 30 Mar, but the draught was not submitted until 20 May.

[97] PRO Adm 95/48, 21 Oct 1816 – presumably as fitted for the Algiers expedition.

[98] PRO Adm1/4020, 23 Dec 1812, refers to the new bombs as *Vesuvius, Terror, Fury* and *Beelzebub*. The Admiralty's habit of allocating names to proposed ships before they were contracted leads to much confusion in the lists of this period: there are, for example, references to bombs of the 1812 programme to be built by Good of Bridport, Bailey of Ipswich and Brindley of Frindsbury, and the name *Thunder* is also mentioned.

[99] PRO Adm 95/48, 21 Oct 1816.

[100] PRO Adm 91/4, 24 Jun 1819.

[101] See Dr A Lambert, *The Last Sailing Battlefleet* (London 1992) for the strategic thinking on this subject.

[102] PRO Adm 95/85, f110.

[103] PRO Adm 95/85, f110.

[104] PRO Adm 95/85, f110.

[105] PRO Adm 95/85, f112.

[106] Tables based on information given in D Wray's articles in *Model Shipwright* 25-27 (1978-79).

[107] PRO WO 46/3, Board of Ordnance Minutes 1695.

[108] PRO WO 46/3, Board of Ordnance Minutes.

[109] PRO WO 46/3, Board of Ordnance Minutes, ff29-33.

[110] PRO WO 46/3, Board of Ordnance Minutes. The next section is based on the digest in the minutes of an investigation into why the bomb vessels were late into service in 1693-94.

[111] NMM SER/81/, 14 Dec 1694 & 19 Apr 1695.

[112] PRO WO 46/3, dated 27 Feb.

[113] Catalogue number 102 in H L Blackmore, *The Armouries of the Tower of London*, illustrated in Plate 64.

[114] PRO Adm1/4018, 24 Aug 1810; the Board of Ordnance withdrew its approval on 23 Dec 1811.

[115] PRO Adm1/4020, 23 Dec 1812.

[116] See David Wray, *Model Shipwright* 27, p26.

[117] This section is based on the Board of Ordnance Minutes which run from 1695 onward in PRO WO 46/-.

[118] PRO WO 46/3, Board of Ordnance Minutes dated 13 Aug 1695.

[119] PRO WO 46/3, f33, dated 1695.

[120] PRO Adm1/4018, 18 Jul 1807.

[121] I am grateful to Mr Brian Lavery for this reference which comes from the Anson papers at Shugborough.

[122] Quoted in A Shirley, 'A very interesting point in geography: the 1773 Phipps Expedition towards the North Pole', *Arctic* 37, No 4 (1984).

Sources

The majority of the information in this book is based on research into the documents held at a number of repositories. A number of near-contemporary and secondary sources have also been consulted.

Draughts

One of the earliest plans of a British bomb is not to be found in the UK, but in the Danish Rigsarkivet. This shows the profile and midships section of what is thought to be the *Mortar* of 1693. Comprehensive draughts are also held of *Terrible* (1730), *Basilisk* (1740) and a ketch which probably represents the *Infernal* of 1757.

List of plans of bomb vessels held at the National Maritime Museum, Greenwich.

Purpose-built vessels

Salamander class	1730	Lines and deck
Alderney class	1734	Lines and profile, deck and midships section
Blast class	1740	As *Alderney*
Comet class	1741	As *Alderney*
Granado class	1741	Lines, profile & decoration
Infernal class	1756	Lines & profile, deck and midships section
Carcass (*Infernal* class)	1758	1768: Deck. 1773: profile & midships section/orlop & upper deck
Ætna (repeat *Infernal* class)	1776	Lines and profile, decks, frame
Project	1805	Lines, profile, deck and sections
Vesuvius class	1812	Lines/profile/orlop/lower deck/upper deck/midships section/specification
Terror (*Vesuvius* class)		1837: fitted for the Arctic: Profile/orlop/lower deck/upper deck/midships section. 1839 Arctic: Profile/orlop/lower deck/propeller aperture
Beelzebub (*Vesuvius* class)		1816: decks
Hecla class	1813	Lines/profile/orlop/lower deck/upper deck/midships section
Fury (*Hecla* class)		1818: Profile/orlop/lower deck/upper deck. 1821: discovery vessel: profile & midships section/orlop/lower deck/upper deck/quarterdeck
Etna (*Hecla* class)		As survey vessel: Profile/orlop/quarterdeck & forecastle
Erebus (*Hecla* class)		Arctic: same as *Terror*
Thunder (*Hecla* class)		As survey vessel 1833: Profile/orlop/lower deck/ upper deck

Bomb vessel conversions

Baltimore	1742	1758: Profile, deck & midships section
Racehorse/*Thunder*	1757	Profile & upper deck, midships section. 1773: fitted for Arctic: lines & profile/ orlop/upper deck/quarterdeck & forecastle
Explosion	1797	As fitted: Lines & profile/ decks & midships section
Hecla	1797	As fitted: Lines & profile/ decks & midships section
Strombolo	1797	As fitted: Profile & midships section
Sulphur	1797	As fitted: Lines & profile/ decks & midships section
Tartarus	1797	As fitted: Lines & profile/ decks & midships section
Volcano	1797	As fitted: Profile & quarterdeck, forecastle & midships section
Discovery	1789	1798: Lines & profile/decks. Conversion to bomb; decks/midships section
Perseus	1775	1798: Profile/lower deck/upper deck & midships section
Bulldog	1781	1798: Profile & midships section
Fury	1790	1798: Profile, profile & midships section, decks and section
Meteor	1803	1803: Profile and sections, decks
Acheron	1803	1803: Profile and sections, decks
Meteor, ex-*Star*	1805	1812: Profile, decks, midship section

Documents

A. National Maritime Museum

The Admiralty collection of plans is fundamental and is listed above.

Dimensions Book A & B. Copies of the originals held at the Public Record Office.

Admiralty Progress Books. Copies of the originals held at the Public Record Office.

Navy Board papers under reference CHA in the NMM manuscript collection.

SER/ Sergison papers.

B. The British Library, Department of Western Manuscripts

Add Manuscripts, 'Dummer's Voyage around the Mediterranean'.

C. Public Record Office

Admiralty

Adm 1. Admiralty In Letters.

Adm 2. Admiralty Out Letters.

Adm 7. Navy Board Estimates.

Adm 8. List of Ships in Sea Pay and their Stations.

Adm 95. Sailing Quality Reports.

Adm 106. Navy Board Correspondence.

Board of Ordnance

WO 44. To the Master General.

WO 46. From the Master General.

WO 47. Board of Ordnance Minutes.

The printed works consulted are fully cited in the end notes.

Index

Page entries in italics refer to illustrations; those in bold refer to tables.